St. Francis Xavier
Catholic Church Records

Marriages and Deaths
1749-1838

Knox County
Indiana

Barbara Schull Wolfe
Organizing Regent, Metamonong Chapter of
The Daughters of the American Revolution
Pulaski County, Indiana

Typed by
Rosalie Looker Rowe

HERITAGE BOOKS
2008

HERITAGE BOOKS
AN IMPRINT OF HERITAGE BOOKS, INC.

Books, CDs, and more—Worldwide

For our listing of thousands of titles see our website
at
www.HeritageBooks.com

Published 2008 by
HERITAGE BOOKS, INC.
Publishing Division
100 Railroad Ave. #104
Westminster, Maryland 21157

Copyright © 1999 Barbara Schull Wolfe

Other books by the author:
St. Francis Xavier Catholic Church Records: Baptisms, 1749-1838, Knox County, Indiana

All rights reserved. No part of this book may be reproduced or transmitted in any form or by any means, electronic or mechanical, including photocopying, recording or by any information storage and retrieval system without written permission from the author, except for the inclusion of brief quotations in a review.

International Standard Book Numbers
Paperbound: 978-0-7884-1140-3
Clothbound: 978-0-7884-7714-0

DEDICATION

This book was compiled because the French fur traders settled Logansport in 1828; it is dedicated the All Saints Parish Priests: Rev. Donald Gross, Rev. Leo Haigerty, and Rev. Alex Paternoster. It is also dedicated to the memory of my loving father, Thomas Levi Schull (1902-1969).

Barbara Schull Wolfe

TABLE OF CONTENTS

Introduction *vii*

List of Abbreviations *x*

Marriage Records of St. Francis Xavier Catholic Church, 1749-1838

    Part One
      Indians & Slaves *1*
      Surnames Alard through Vital *2*
      Deceased Spouses *26*

    Part Two
      Surnames Alarie to Wire *30*
      Deceased Spouses *44*
      Cross Reference of Names *45*

Parental Information from Marriage Records, 1749-1838 *47*

Death Records of St. Francis Xavier Catholic Church, 1749-1838

    Surnames Unknown & Indians *73*
    Slaves *74*
    Surnames Alard to Wilson *76*

INTRODUCTION

The history of Vincennes, Indiana is a direct creation of the empire builders of Europe. France, England, and Spain all wanted their share of the New World spoils. Spain was seeking gold and instant wealth as well as bringing new souls to God. England was searching for wealth and great farmlands. France was searching for wealth through the fur trade and a great desire to convert the Native Americans to Christianity.

The French explorers and settlers remained mostly in the northlands because of the fear of the Iroquois tribes. Finally, Robert Cavelier, Sieur de La Salle came to the New World. He had studied assiduously the reports of exploration and had learned several Indian languages in preparation for exploration for his king.

La Salle sold everything he possessed and collected 14 men and 4 canoes to begin his exploration in 1669. The early records of his adventures have been lost, but it is known that sometime in his explorations he entered the Wabash Country and floated down the Oubache.

It is known from historical records that he entered what is now Indiana in 1671-72 via the Lake Michigan, St. Joseph River and the Kankakee River on his way toward the Mississippi River.

After La Salle's adventures of discovery, the only European

visitors were the coureurs de bois, who were wandering traders and fur trappers. Occasionally a priest would visit the area to work with the trappers and Indians. The English began making settlements beyond the Applachians which triggered the French consciousness into building forts in the Wabash Country.

The first fort was Post Ouiatanon which is near present day Lafayette. There were several Ouiatanon villages in the vicinity and the rapids in the Wabash made it a natural stopping point for transfer of furs and supplies from pirogues to canoes. Fort Miamis was built near the present day Fort Wayne principally to watch for English incursions into French territory. Vincennes and Terre Haute were forts, supply stations and fur collection points. The three forts were begun in the early 1700's.

Tradition indicates that several priests visited the Vincennes settlement in the early 1700's, but the first parish records date from 1749 when the first log church was erected in the settlement by Father Meurin. The Bishop of Quebec, who had jurisdiction over the Wabash Country, sent several priests to the area. Because of an acute shortage of priests, Vincennes was without a priest for 7 years until Father Gibault was sent in 1770. The second church was erected by Father Gibault in 1786

Little had changed in the Wabash Country from the time the

outposts were built until the Treaty of Paris was concluded in 1763. The British then controlled the whole western area. The American Revolution had little effect on Vincennes until George Rogers Clark initiated his attack and captured the fort for the Colonies. Father Gibault had abetted Clark in the effort of defeating the British. The French of Vincennes proclaimed their allegiance to the new government

Vincennes became under the jurisdiction of Bishop Carroll of the new Colonial Union. Then the Diocese of Bardstown, Kentucky was created with the Wabash Country being part of that Diocese. As the population increased a new diocese was created in the Wabash Country. The Vincennes Diocese came into being under the leadership of Bishop Simon Gabriel de Remur Brute' in 1836.

Richard B. Copeland
September 15, 1998

ABBREVIATIONS

c/o	*child of*
s/o	*son of*
d/o	*daughter of*
w/o	*wife of*
illeg	*illegitimate*
b.	*born*
bpt	*baptized*
d.	*died*
dit	*called*
-----	name unknown
m.	*married*
( )	*supposition in names or found in register*

ST. FRANCIS XAVIER CATHOLIC CHURCH

MARRIAGE RECORDS

1749 - 1838

PART I

INDIANS:

Angelique -to- Genier, Honre   5-18-1814

Cecil -to- Barron, Joseph   2-11-1798
Chaganon, Antoine -to- Sghghigrita, Marie   7-3-1749
Chicamicge, Marie Anne (widow of Antoine Marie -to- Butos,
                          Jean Baptiste   4-20-1750
Geapechagane Le Petite, Pierre -to- Mgkicge, Catherine   6-26-1749

Ipsue, Marie Louise -to- Berthiome, Noel   8-19-1799

Le Petite, Pierre Geapechane -to-Mgkicge, Catherine   6-26-1749
Louis of the nation of Pous, Chief -to- Marie Angelique of the skies
                          6-9-1795
Marie Louise, Chicksaw indian -to- Joseph, Paducah Indian   8-10-1751
Mgkicge, Catherine -to- Le Petite, Pierre Geapickagane confered
                          6-26-1749
Marieva, Piankichias indian -to- Levron dit Metayer, Louis   7-10-1787

Paducah indian, Joseph -to- Chicksaw indian, Marie Louise   8-10-1751

Sgnghigrita - Illinoise, Marie -to- Chaganon, Antoine   7-3-1740

SLAVES:

Joseph and Charlotte of Toussaint la Framboise   5-20-175X
Joseph a Pucah and Charlotte od Sir Antoine La Framoise   12-5-1758
Susanne and Joseph of Mr. Cripen   7-12-1760

Alard, Louis
   Pethier, Catherine (widow Beket)   9-20-1784
Amelin, Jean
   Gaudere, Francoise   3-2-1829
Amelin, Joseph
   Gariepe, Poerdret Marie Anne   1-25-1773
Amelin, Laurent
   Lagarde, Marie Louise   5-21-1798
Amelin, Marie
   Cartier, Joseph   10-22-1827
Andray, Agathe
   Dclisle, Charles   2-2-1800
Andray, Pierre
   Boulon, Josette   7-16-1798
Andre, Louise
   Bozer, Jean Baptist   2-3-1794
Andre, Marianne
   Charon, Augustin   5-5-1785
Andre, Marianne
   Barrois, Francois   8-7-1826
Andre, Therese
   Theriaque, Michel   1-7-1796
Antara, Marie Josephe
   Querre, Pierre   10-17-1763
Arpin, Francois Poitvin dit
   Chartier, Genevieve   6-2-1794
Aveline, Laurent
   Du Devoir, Marie   5-28-1808

Babini, Michel Ange (widower of Marie Wiron)
   Le Grand, Delle Veronique   7-1-1788
Baillargeon, Nicolas
   Valle, Pelagie   5-23-1808
Baillargeons, Nicolas ?
   Plisson, Francoiae (widow of Jean Bte Demers) 7-24-1778
Balairjon, Archange
   Sans Soucison or Sans Souci, Joseph   10-1-1810
Balairjon, Barbe
   Languedoc, Andre   10-1-1810
Barada, Antoine
   Desrosiers, Marguerite   10-23-1759
Barbau, Francois
   Deganne, Archeange   5-15-1808
Baril, Francois
   De Bois, Marie Louise   8-30-1786
Barnabi, Antoine
   Laviollette, Marie   8-8-1825
Baron   see also : Barron - Barrois
Baron, Joseph (widower of Barbe Brouiellet)
   Gamelin, Josephine   5-21-1808
Barrios   see also Barron - Baron
Barrios, Angelique
   Tougas, Guillaume   8-7-1826

Barrois, Francois
   Godere, Victorie 2-2-1801
Barrois, Francois
   Andre, Marianne 8-7-1826
Barrois, J. Marie (groom)
   Gamelin, Adelaide 8-2-1824
Barrois, Lambert
   Danis, Marie Louise 2-23-1789
Barrois, Lambert (widower of Marie Louise Danis)
   Bono, Angelique (widow of Pierre Querie dit Latulipe) 4-6-1795
Barron see also Barrois - Baron
Barron, Joseph
   Cecile, indian 2-11-1798
Barron, Joseph (widower of Cecile, indian)
   Brouillet, Barbe (widow of Laurent Giroult) 2-11-1803
Barsalow, Jean Baptist
   Millet, Rosalie 8-20-1798
Barsalow, Magdaline
   Delisle, Charles 4-18-1785
Bayargeon, Pelagie (bride)
   Page, Dominique 11-29-1828
Bayarion, Francoise
   Moyse, Charles 5-23-1796
Beaulon, Amisble
   Gaudere, Marie Josephe 1-26-1763 (sic) 1773
Beaulon, Hypolite
   Des Bois, Magdaline 9-28-1786
Belin, Marie Josephe
   Estiv, Joseph 6-24-1753
Benae, Chartier, Jean Baptist
   Toulon, dit Genichon, Marie 11-8-1813
Benas, dit Chartier, Marie Louise
   Deneau, Toussaint 11-8-1813
Bequet, Francoise
   Gendron, Jean Baptist 7-25-1796
Bergan, Catherine
   St. Aubin, Louis 4-16-1787
Bergant, Charles
   Dany, Marguerite 8-2-1784
Berthiaume, Angelique
   Valiquet, Francis 8-2-1784
Berthiome, Noel
   Ipsue, Marie Louise (indian) 8-19-1799
Berton, dit St. Martin, Jean Baptist
   Perodet, Barbe 4-28-1788
Bezaillon, Benoit
   Choteau, Marie Julie 4-20-1806
Bequet, Cecile
   Daigniaux, Louis Toussaint 1-24-1791
Benaque, Joseph Chartier dit (widower of Marie Louise Girardo
   Renault, Charlotti 10-20-1793
Bisaillon, Francoise Bernice
   Picardand, Alexis 3-2-1827
Bissonet, Marie (widow of Toussaint De Noyon)
   Poirier, dit Delege, Pierre 10-17-1785

Bollon, Susanne
   Gauder, Pierre   5-5-1760
Boneau, Frances
   Valle, Alexander   8-2-1784
Boneau, Jean Baptist
   Desrosier, Pelagie   10-1-1810
Bonhomme, Eleanore
   Desjean, Alexis   2-23-1829
Bonhomme, Jean Baptist
   Villeneuve, Geneieve   4-15-1793
Bonhomme, J. Baptiste
   Tougas, Susanne   1-4-1830
Bonneau   see also Bono
Bonneau, Angelique (widow of Francois Bazinet)
   De Frontenac, Pierre Tierie   2-4-1788
Bonneau, Anne
   Dubois, Toussain   10-6-1788
Bonneau, Geneieve
   Villeneuve, Charles   1-14-1773
Bonneau, Geneieve (widow of Charles Villeneuve)
   Coloutre, Jean Baptist   3-4-1799
Bonneau, Jean Baptiste
   Pacanne, Marie   11-6-1786
Bonneau, Lambert
   Boyer, Marianne   8-10-1824
Bonneau, Marie
   Godere, Francois   1-30-1804
Bonneau, Pierre
   Cournoyer, Heleine   9-19-1785
Bono   see also Bonneau
Bono, Angelique (widow of Pierre Querie dit Latulipe)
   Barrois, Lambert (widower of Marie Louise Danis) 4-6-1795
Bono, Auguste
   Mizot,   (bride)   4-6-1795
Bordelau, see also Bourdeloux - Bourdeleau
Bordelau, Antoine
   Caron, Catherine   1-29-1758
Bordelau, Archange
   Sanson, Alexander   10-3-1785
Bordelau, Catherine
   Girardin, Auguste   5-23-1808
Bordeleau, Marie Magdeleine
   Renault, Jean Baptiste   7-9-1779
Bordeleau, Michel
   Le Cointe, Ursule   7-3-1786
Bordeleau, Pierre
   Gaudere, Therese   10-24-1825
Bordeleau, Ursule
   Languedoc, Charles   5-10-1808
Bosseron, Rose
   Marchal, Antoine   5-22-1797
Bosseron, Suzanne
   Fortin, Louis Nicolas   1-3-1801

Boucher, Amable Vital
    Mallet, Angelique Marie   5-3-1824
Boucher, Jean Baptiste
    Cartier, Marie Magdalene   9-17-1811
Boucher, Joseph
    Tremblai, Archange   6-13-1814
Boucher, Julie
    Brouillet, Pierre   6-13-1814
Boucher, Vital
    Cardinal, Marie Joseph   5-2-1785
Boulon, Josette
    Andray, Pierre   7-16-1798
Bourdelau   see also Bordelau - Bourdeloux
Bourdeleau, Michel
    Cournoier, Angelique   10-26-1825
Bourdeloux   see also Bordelau - Bourdeleau
Bourdeloux, Francoise
    Giroux, Louis   (May?) 1827
Bourdeloux, Ignace
    Campau, Francois   2-14-1825
Boye, Francois
    Sequin dit La Deroute, Barbe   4-24-1792
Boyer, F. Xavier
    Grimard, Modeste   1-10-1826
Boyer, Francois
    Sequien, Barbe   5-17-1808
Boyer, Jean Baptiste
    Andre, Louise   2-3-1794
Boyer. Josephine
    Dardeine, Jean Augustine   1-18-1830
Boyer, Louis
    La Pointe, Catherine   1-8-1789
Boyer, Marianne
    Bonneau, Lambert   8-10-1824
Boyer, Marie Louise
    Touga, Alexandre   8-21-1826
Boyer, Ursule
    Dubois, Joseph   8-4-1794
Boymir, Marie
    Grimard, Joseph   11-3-1824
Brossard, Joseph
    Millot, Felicite   2-23-1789
Brouillet, Barbe
    Giroud, Laurent   7-4-1796
Brouillet, Barbe (widow of Laurent Girourd)
    Barron, Joseph   2-11-1803
Brouillet, Michel
    Richardville, Marie   9-21-1811
Brouillet, Pierre
    Boucher, Julie   6-13-1814
Butler, Joseph
    Jenkins, Julie Jane   12-3-1829
Butos, Jean Baptiste
    Chicamicge, Marie Anne - indian - (widow Antoine Marie) 4-20-1750

Cabassier, Charles
    Mallet, Marie Louise   1-30-1792
Cabassier, Pierre
    Malet, Francoise   11-20-1797
Cadoret, Francois
    Godere, Marie Louise   1-28-1802
Cadoret, Louis
    Cardinal, Constance   11-2-1830
Caillou, Amable
    Rascicot, Francoise   2-16-1828 ? 1829
Caloutre, Jean Baptiste
    Bonneau, Geneieve (widow of Charles Villeneive) 3-4-1799
Campau, Francoise
    Bourdeloux, Ignace   2-14-1825
Campeau, Francois
    Grimard, Heleine   5-8-1786
Campeau, Heleine
    Ravalet, Louis   10-1-1810
Campeau, Jeanne
    Rolus, Samuel   10-1-1810
Campeau, Susanne
    Geroux, Louis   5-31-1830
Campeau, Geneieve
    Cardinal, Jean Bte   12-11-1809
Campos, Catherine
    Gauder, Rene   3-3-176X
Cardinal, Barbe
    Pelletier, Pierre   7-15-1805
Cardinal, Celeste (widow of Joseph Levron)
    Joyeux, Joseph   6-13-1796
Cardinal, Constance
    Cadoret, Louis   11-2-1830
Cardinal, Felicite (widow of Francois Trotier)
    Soudrietta, Charles   10-1-1810
Cardinal, Francois
    Jacob, Marguerite   5-23-1808
Cardinal, Henrietta
    Lognen, Louis   10-1-1810
Cardinal, James
    Edyline, Barbe   8-2-1784
Cardinal, Jeanne (widow of Jean Baptiste Touga)
    Montplaiser, Andre   4-10-1795
Cardinal, Joseph
    Crely, Francoise   11-26-1806
Cardinal, Joseph
    Querre, or Kerry, Elizabeth   10-19-1829
Cardinal, Marie
    Dubois, Etienne   11-23-1806
Cardinal, Marie Felicite
    Trottier, Francois   1-2-1792
Cardinal, Jean Bte
    Campeau, Geneieve   12-11-1809
Cardinal, Marie Francoise
    Levry, dit Martin, Pierre   2-19-1787

Cardinal, Marie Jeanne	
Touga, Joseph	1-16-1773
Cardinal, Marie Josephe	
Boucher, Vital	5-2-1785
Cardinal, Nicolas	
Girard, Marie	1-4-1761
Cardinal, Nicolas	
Danis, Ursule	5-10-1808
Cardinal, Therese	
Vachet dit St. Antoine, Francois	5-2-1785
Caron, Catherine	
Bordelau, Antoine	1-29-1758
Caron, Louise	
Lefebvre, Antoine	1-25-1751
Caron, Marie	
Potevin, Joseph	7-22-1828
Cartier, Celeste	
Turpin, Louis	5-24-1830
Cartier, Isador	
Joyeuse, Celeste	1-11-1824
Cartier, Joseph	
Amelin, Marie	10-22-1827
Cartier, Marie Magdalene	
Boucher, Jean Baptiste	9-17-1811
Cartier, Pierre	
L'Allemand, Heleine	2-10-1770
Cartier, Pierre	
Mallet, Veronique	4-12-1790
Cartier or Kirky, Susanne (widow of Laiumiere)	
Russel, Robert Woodburn	9-12-1828
Cayon, Francois	
Potevin, Marie	7-24-1797
Chabot, Bernard	
Renaud, Therese	5-15-1808
Chabot, Cecile	
Racine, Andre	5-21-1793
Chabot, Joseph	
Clermont, Ursule (widow of Francois LeCointe DeComte)	1-18-1773
Chamberlan, dit Germaine, Therese	
Cornouillier, Antoine	9-24-1810
Chapard, Antoine	
Denoyan, Barbe	11-19-1806
Chapart, Ambroise	
Seguien, Agathe	11-3-1813
Chapart, Marie Claire	
Vaudrie, John Baptiste	6-20-1785
Chapart, Nicholas	
Lacoste, Cecilia	7-19-1784
Charon, Augustin	
Andre, Marianne	5-5-1785
Chartier, Geneieve	
Poitevin, dit Arpin, Francois	6-2-1794
Chartier, Jean Baptiste Benae	
Toulon dit Genichon, Marie	11-8-1813

Chartier dit Binaque, Joseph (widower of Marie Louise Gerardo)
    Renault, Charlotte   10-20-1793
Chartier, Joseph (widower of Charlotte Renault)
    Perron, Geneieve (widow of Jean Potevin)   1-26-1803
Chartier, Marie Louis Benas dit
    Denneau, Toussiant   11-8-1813
Chatagney, Ignace
    Perron, Marie   3-19-1790
Choteau, Marie Julie
    Bezaillon, Benoit   4-20-1806
Clermont, Marie Louise (widow of Guillaume Daperon)
    Tetro, Jean Baptiste   11-28-1787
Clermont, Ursule (widow of ---- DeComte)
    Chabot, Joseph   1-18-1773
Codenoir, Louis Preville dit
    Mallet, Theresa   5-8-1786
Codere, Louis
    Levron, Elisabeth   2-8-1770
Codere, Marguatite
    Delorier, Louis   8-2-1784
Codere, Rene
    St. Germaine, Felicity   2-13-1786
Colon, Geneieve (widow of Pierre Grimard)
    Oullet, John Baptiste (widower of Geneieve Guibord) 9-14-1785
Compagnet, Pierre
    Gamelin, Marguerite   5-28-1808
Compagnot, Francoise
    Rasicot, Francois   1-23-1800
Compagnot, Marianne
    Huno, Gabriel   1-21-1799
Compagnot, Marie Anne
    Racine St. Marie, Francois   11-15-1787
Compagnot, Marie Therese
    Gauderr, Francois   1-18-1773
Compagnotte, Eustache
    Mallet, Marie Anne   1-17-1829 license
Compagnotte, Marie Anne
    Laplante, Hyacinthe   6-1-1830
Compagnotte, Pierre
    Rejimbald, Henene   6-20-1830
Cornouiller, Victoire Trempe dit
    Dejean, Phillipe   7-21-1794
Cornouller, Angelique
    Mallet, Ambroise   9-6-1811
Cornouillier, Antoine
    Chamberlan dit Germaine, Therese   9-24-1810
Coulter, Elene
    Roux, Emanuel   9-5-1825
Cournoier, Angelique
    Bourdelcau, Michel   10-26-1825
Cournouiller, Geneieve (widow of Pierre Latour)
    Moyse, Jean Baptiste (widower of Geneieve Grimard) 10-1-1810
Cournoyer, Clemente
    Richarville, Antoine Derouet dit   5-31-1830

Cournoyer, Geneieve
    La Toure, Pierre   2-13-1786
Cournoyer, Heleine
    Bonneau, Pierre   9-19-1785
Cournoyer, Marie Anne
    Denau, Charles   10-10-1828
Cournoyer, Pierre
    Page, Marie   7-13-1829
Cournozier, Ambroise
    Du Devoir, Geneieve   12-1-1806
Crely, Francoise
    Cardinal, Joseph   11-26-1806
Crepaux, Louis
    Perthius, Louise   11-26-1749
Crepeau, Catherine
    Tougas, Jean Baptiste   1-18-1773
Custeaud, Jean Baptiste
    Larche, Marguerite   11-28-1802
Custos, Marie (widow of Levron dit Mitteller)
    La Coste, Andre   1-25-1773

Dagenay, Sr Ambrose
    Outlas, Dame Francoise (widow of Antoine Droit De Richarville)
         1-21-1773
Dagenay, Victoire
    Rene, Joseph Gabriel   6-13-1803
Daher, Elizabeth
    Rene, Joseph   5-23-1808
Daigniaux, Louis Toussaint
    Bequet, Cecile   1-24-1791
Dalbe, Antoine
    Villeneuve, Marie   7-30-1826
Damilde, Elizabeth Catherine
    Gaudere, Charles   10-26-1829
Danis, Marie Louise
    Barrois, Lambert   2-23-1789
Danis, Ursule
    Cardinal, Nicolas   5-10-1808
Dany, Marguerite
    Bergant, Charles   8-2-1784
Daplond, Guillame
    Fausement?, Susanne Therese(widow of Jean Toulon dit
                       Ganichon)   4-4-1796
Dardeine, Jean Augustin
    Boyer, Josephine   1-18-1830
Darden, Augustin
    Godere, Jeannette   9-13-1824
De Frontenac, Pierre Tierie
    Bonneau, Angelique (widow of Francois Bazinet) 2-4-1788
De Gane, Archange
    Laforet, Pierre   8-16-1802
De Gane, Joseph
    La Feuillade, Marianne (widow of St. Aubin) 8-5-1799

Deganne, Archeange Barbau, Francois	5-15-1808
De Ganne, Joseph Ravalette, Madeline	11-29-1790
Dejarlais, Eloi La Tremoville, Marie	5-23-1808
Dejean, Phillipe Trampe dit Cornouailler, Victoire	7-21-1794
Delaurier, Adelaide Racine Francois	7-26-1824
Delaurier, Pierre Renau dit Ravalet, Theresa	11-11-1813
Deligne, Marie Louise Joyeuse, Joseph	2-15-1791
Delile, Charlotte Loyon, Charles	7-14-1793
Delile, Marie Josephine Grimard, Pierre	4-6-1795
Delisle, Cecile Noval, Hypolithe	5-28-1808
Delisle, Charles Barsalou, Magdalene	4-18-1785
Delisle, Charles Andray, Agathe	2-2-1800
Delisle, Victoire O'Neille, Joseph	12-25-1809
Delorier, Joseph Lefevre, Marie Louise	2-22-1830
Delorier, Louis Codere, Marguarite	8-2-1784
De Mers-Dumais, Pierre Ouillete, Agate	2-25-1775
Denau, Charles Cournoyer, Marie Anne	10-10-1828
Deneau, Francoise Vachet, Francois	5-30-1808
Deneau, Touissant Denoyan, Angelique	11-19-1806
Deneau, Toussaint Benas dit Chartier, Marie Louise	11-8-1813
Denie, Marie Louise St. Aubin, Jean Baptiste	10-19-1760
Denoyan, Angelique Deneau, Toussaint	11-19-1806
Denoyan, Barbe Chapard, Antoine	11-19-1806
De Noyan, Francoise Godere, Henri Pierre	7-9-1798
Denoyan, Jean Louis Pellu, Marie Amable	1-19-1761
Desbiens, Andre Rochard, Helene	1-24-1803
Desbiens, Helene Rejembald dit Jerome, Antoine	7-19-1828

Des Bois, Magdalene
   Beaulon, Hypolite   9-28-1786
Des Bois, Marie Louise
   Baril, Francois   8-30-1786
Desjardins, Hiacynthe
   Page, Madeleine   1-24-1803
Desjean, Alexis
   Bonhomme, Eleonore   2-23-1829
Desloriez, Desanges Renaud dit (bride)
   Touga, Guillaume   7-6-1801
Desloriez, Eleanore Renaud dit
   Touga, Auguste   7-6-1801
Desloriez, Geneieve Renaud dit
   Edeline, Francois Xavier Joseph   2-18-1799
Desnaux, Rene
   Seguin, Cecile   2-10-1800
Des Noyons, Marguerite
   Sevigny, Eustachw   4-27-1806
Desrochers, Joseph
   Perron, Jeanne   2-27-1770
Desrosier, Pelagie
   Boneau, Jean Baptiste   10-1-1810
Desrosiers, Marguerite
   Barada, Antoine   10-23-1759
Desvegnets, Dame Mares (widow of Sr Charles Lefebvre)
   Le Grasm John Marie (widower of Dame Marie Jane Gamelin)
                                                               7-18-1779
Detailly, Joseph
   La Belle, Catherine   10-16-1786
Devegnais, Marie Anne
   Mayot or Maillot, Nicolas   8-3-1789
De Villera, Marie Joseph
   Petit dit La Luniere, Antoine   2-29-1787
Dion dit Guitard, Pierre (widower of Marie Monique Morant)
   Poirier, Marie Joseph (widow of Dominique Bergan) 3-26-1788
Drouet de Richardville see: Richardvill - Richarville
Duboise, Barbe
   St. Marie, Henri   2-12-1827 license
Duboise, Charles
   Moyse, Susanne   6-16-1828
Duboise, Etienne
   Cardinal, Marie   11-23-1806
Duboise, Jeanette
   Noyse, Joseph   1-19-1829
Duboise, Joseph
   Boyer, Ursule   8-4-1794
Duboise, Toussain
   Bonneau, Anne   10-6-1788
Du Devoir, Anne
   Racine, Jean Baptiste   11-23-1756
Du Devoir, Barbe
   Oisi, Michel   8-23-1763
Du Devoir, Geneieve
   Cournoyier, Ambroise   12-1-1806

Du Devoir, Marie
    Aveline, Laurent   5-28-1808
Du Mais or De Mers, Pierre
    Ouilette, Agate   2-25-1775
Dupre, Louis
    St. Antoine, Therese   2-16-1801

Edeline, Francois Xavier Joseph
    Renaud dit Desloriez, Geneieve   2-18-1799
Edeline, Marie Josepte
    Perrot, Nicolas   7-24-1778
Edeline, Nicolas
    Godore, Therese   8-10-1795
Edyline, Barbe
    Cardinal, James   8-2-1784
Emeline, Marianne (widow of Joseph De La Feuillade)
    La Forest, Pierre   2-10-1770
Estev, Joseph
    Belin, Marie Josephe   6-24-1753

Fausement ?, Susanne Therese (widow of Jean Toulon dit Ganchion)
    Daplond, Guillame   4-4-1796
Fevel, Josephte
    Ravalet, Louis   8-2-1784
Fiot, Joseph
    Galvin, Elizabeth   5-23-1808
Fortin, Louis Nicolas
    Bosseron, Suzanne   1-3-1801
Frederick, Catherine
    Querry, Antoine   1-2-1824

Galvin, Elizabeth
    Fiot, Joseph   5-23-1808
Gamelin, Adelaide (bride)
    Barrois, J. Marie   8-2-1824
Gamelin, Antoine (widower of Catherine Gamelin)
    Hunot, Magdeleine   8-20-1787
Gamelin, Josephine
    Baron, Joseph (widower of Barbe Brouillet)   5-21-1808
Gamelin, Marguerite
    Compagnet, Pierre   5-28-1808
Gamelin, Paul
    Richerville, Marguerite Drouet De   6-6-1785
Gamelin, Pierre
    Vaudry, Ursule   7-24-1778
Gamenin or Gamelin, Pierre
    Villeneure, Francoise   11-11-1813
Garcia, Jean (spaniard)
    La Rue, Catherine   11-19-1788
Gauder, Pierre
    Bollon, Susanne   5-5-1760

Gauder, Rene	
Campos, Catherine	3-3-176X
Gaudere, Alexis	
Villeneuve, Felicite	9-22-1829
Gaudere, Charles	
Damilde, Elizabeth Catherine	10-26-1829
Gaudere, Felicite	
Valeix, Alexandre (widow of Fracoise Boneau)	5-23-1793
Gaudere, Francoise	
Amelin, Jean	3-2-1829
Gaudere, Marie Joseph	
Beaulon, Aimable	1-26-1763 (sic) (1773)?
Gaudere, Therese	
Bordeleau, Pierre	10-25-1825
Gaudere, Victoire	
La Feuillade, Pierre	7-14-1795
Gauderr, Francois	
Compagnot, Marie Therese	1-18-1773
Gendron, Jean Baptiste	
Beguet, Francoise	7-25-1796
Genier, Honore	
Angelique (indian)	5-18-1814
Gerard, Marie Joseph (widow of Nicholas Cardinal)	
Lonicont, Francois	3-5-1791
Geroux, Louis	
Campeau, Susanne	5-31-1830
Girard, Marie	
Cardinal, Nicolas	1-4-1761
Girardin, Auguste	
Bordelau, Catherine	5-23-1808
Giroud, Laurent	
Brouillet, Barbe	7-4-1796
Giroux, Andre	
Languedoc, Therese	6-16-1829
Giroux, Louis	
Bourdeloux, Francoise	May? 1827
Goder, Victoire	
Langlois, Jean Baptiste	7-15-1805
Godere, Francois	
Bonneau, Marie	1-30-1804
Godere, Geneieve	
La Buxiere, Charles Joseph	2-13-1786
Godere, Henri Pierre	
De Noyan, Francoise	7-9-1798
Godere, Jeanette	
Darden, Augustin	9-13-1824
Godere, Marie Louise	
Cadoret, Francois	1-28-1802
Godere, Victoire	
Barrois, Francois	2-2-1801
Godore, Therese	
Edeline, Nicolas	8-10-1795
Gonzales, Simon	
Page, Marie	2-27-1798

Goyau, Antoine
    Mieyet, Marie Louise   11-29-1830
Grimard, Charles
    Turpin, Rosalie   12-19-1809
Grimard, Geneieve
    Moise, Jean Baptiste   7-6-1795
Grimard, Heleine
    Campeau, Francois   5-8-1786
Grimard, Joseph
    Boymer, Marie   11-3-1824
Grimard, Marie
    Valle, Rayait   1-4-1830
Grimard, Modeste
    Boyer, F. Xavier   1-10-1826
Grimard, Pierre
    Delile, Marie Josephine   4-6-1795
Guele, Charles
    Jacqueau, Marie Helene   4-4-1796
Guelle, Josephine
    Turpin, Francois   7-14-1805
Guelle, Marie
    Metai, Joseph   11-8-1813
Guinel, Francois
    La Fontaine, Marguerite   6-29-1794
Guitard, Pierre Dion dit (widower of Marie Monique Morant)
    Poirer, Marie Joseph (widow of Dominique Bergan) 3-26-1788

Harvin, Jean
    Mallet, Rose   7-19-1793
Habert, Angelique
    Racine, Francois   7-27-1829
Haneau, Marie Victoire (widow of Antoine Villeray)
    Page, Guillaumw   7-26-1778
Huno, Gabriel
    Compagnot, Mariannw   1-21-1799
Hunot, Magdeline
    Gamelin, Antoine (widower of Catherine Gamelin) 8-20-1787

Ipsue, Marie Louise (indian tribe of Charakis)
    Berthiome, Noel   8-19-1799

Jacob, Marguerite
    Cardinal, Francois   5-23-1808
Jacqueau, Marie Helene
    Guele, Charles   4-4-1796
Jenkins, Julie Ann
    Butler, Joseph   12-3-1829
Jerome, Antoine Rejembald dit
    Desbiens, Helene   7-19-1828
Joyeuse, Celeste
    Cartier, Isadore   1-11-1824

Joyeuse, Guillaume
    Latour, Josette   5-17-1830
Joyeuse, Joseph
    Deligne, Marie Louise   2-15-1791
Joyeux, Joseph
    Cardinal, Celeste (widow of joseph Levron)   6-13-1796

Kieky   see: Cartier, Susanne
Kerrie   see: Querre
Kerry or Querre, Elizabeth
    Cardinal, Joseph   10-19-1829
Kerry, John B.   (Cary)
    Tougas, Susanne   5-31-1830

La Belle, Catherine
    Detailly, Joseph   10-16-1786
La Buniere, Charles Joseph
    Godere, Geneieve   2-13-1786
La Coste, Andre
    Custos, Marie (widow of Leveon dit Mitteller)   1-25-1773
La Coste, Angelique
    Peltier, Andre   1-18-1773
Lacoste, Cecilia
    Chapart, Nicholas   7-19-1784
La Deroute, Barbe Sequin dit
    Boye, Francois   4-24-1792
Lafeuillade, Angelique
    Lionois, Jean Baptiste   8-2-1784
La Feuillade, Charlotte
    Mate, Joseph
La Feuillade, Marianne (widow of Louis Bergeron)
    St. Aubin, Claude   7-17-1797
La Feuillade, Marianne
    De Gane, Joseph   8-5-1799
La Feuillade, Pierre
    Gaudere, Victoire   7-14-1795
Laffont, Dlle Marie
    Mc Cay, Robert   4-18-1786
La Fontaine, Catherine
    Tessier or Texier, Francois   6-29-1795
La Fontaine, Marguerite
    Guinel, Francois   6-29-1794
La Forest, Pierre
    Emelin, Marianne (widow of Joseph dela Feuillade)   2-10-1770
Laforet, Pierre
    De Gane, Archange   8-16-1802
Lagarde, Marie
    Mellieur, Francois   9-9-1811
Lagarde, Marie Louise
    Amelin, Laurent   5-21-1798
La Grand, Delle Veronique
    Babini, Michel Ange (widower of Marie Wiron)   7-1-1788

L'Allemand, Heleine	
Cartier, Pierre	2-10-1770
La Luniere, Antoine Prtit dit	
De Villers, Marie Joseph	2-29-1787
Lamote, Joseph	
Pagix, Marie Joseph	11-24-1793
Lamoureux, Magdeleine St. Germain	
Paille, Joseph	3-19-1770
Langlois, Jannete	
Valle, Alexandre	10-26-1795
Langlois, Jean Baptiste	
Goder, Victoire	7-15-1805
Languedoc, Andre	
Baliarjon, Barbe	10-1-1810
Languedoc, Charles	
Bordeleau, Ursule	5-10-1808
Languedoc, Therese	
Giroux, Andre	6-16-1829
Lapierre dit German, Marguerite	
Malboeuf, Jean Moise	10-3-1788
Laplante, Hyacinthe	
Compagnotte, Marie Anne	6-1-1830
Laplante, Julie	
Tougas, Auguste	1-4-1830
La Pointe, Catherine	
Boyer, Louis	1-8-1789
Larche, Marguerite	
Custeaud, Jean Baptiste	11-28-1802
La Rue, Catherine	
Garcia, Jean (spaniard)	11-19-1788
Latour, Josette	
Joyeuse, Guillaume	2-13-1786
La Toure, Pierre	
Cournoyer, Geneieve	2-13-1786
La Tremouille, Jacque Millet dit	
Tarte, Julie	2-14-1771
La Tremouille, Marie	
Dejarlais, Eloi	5-23-1808
La Tulippe, Thierie , Marie Joseph	
Lefevre, Antoine	1-21-1788
La Violette, Louis Roussian dit	
Poineau, Marie Anne	2-4-1788
Laviollette, Marie	
Barnabi, Antoine	8-8-1825
La Violette, Marie Therese Roufiance dit	
Perron, Pierre	1-26-1773
Le Cointe, Ursule	
Bodeleau, Michel	7-3-1786
Lefebvre, Antoine	
La Tulippe Thierie, Marie Joseph	1-21-1788
Lefevre, Marie Louise	
Delorier, Joseph	2-22-1830
Le Gras, John Marie (widower of Marie Jane Gamelin)	
Desvefneta, Marie (widow of Charles Lefebvre)	7-18-1779

Levron, Elisabeth
    Codere, Louis   2-8-1770
Levron dit Metayer, Louis
    Marieve, Peankickias (indian)   7-10-1787
Levry dit Martin, Pierre
    Cardinal, Marie Francois   2-19-1787
Lionis, Jean Baptiste
    Lafeuillade, Angelique   8-2-1784
Lognen, Louis
    Cardinal, Henriette   10-1-1810
Lonicant, Francois
    Gerard, Marie Joseph (widow of Nicholas Cardinal) 3-5-1791
Loyon, Charles
    Delile, Charlotte   7-14-1793

McCay, Robert
    Laffont, Dlle Marie   4-18-1786

Maillot or Mayot, Nicolas
    Devegnais, Marie Anne   8-3-1789
Malboeuf, Jean Moise
    Lapierre dit German, Marguerite   10-3-1788
Malet, Francoise
    Cabassier, Pierre   11-20-1797
Mallet, Ambroise
    Cornoullier, Angelique   9-6-1811
Mallet, Angelique
    Roux, Pierre   1-20-1794
Mallet, Angelique Marie
    Boucher, Amable Vital   5-3-1824
Mallet, Elizabeth
    Richard, Jean Baptiste   2-27-1786
Mallet, Louis
    Querre, Geneieve   5-23-1808
Mallet, Marguerite
    Tiriacque, Jacques   11-3-1829
Mallet, Marie Ann
    Compagnetti, Eustache   1-17-1829 license
Mallet, Marie Louise
    Cabassier, Charles   1-30-1792
Mallet, Rose
    Harvin, Jean   7-19-1793
Mallet, Theresa
    Preville dit Codenoir, Louis   5-8-1786
Mallet, Therese
    Renault, Jean Baptist   10-27-1750
Mallet, Veronique
    Cartier, Pierre   4-12-1790
Mangin, Marie Louise
    Menan, Pierre   1-28-176X
Marchal, Antoine
    Bosseron, Rose   5-22-1797

Martin, Pierre Levry dit
    Cardinal, Marie Francoise   2-19-1787
Mate, Joseph
    La Feuillade, Charlotte   7-24-1786
Mayot or Maillot, Nicolas
    Devegnais, Marie Anne   8-3-1789
Meenis, Marie Joseph Polly (widow of Jean Meenis)
    Tremont, Jean   8-22-1801
Mellieur, Francois
    Lagarde, Marie   9-9-1811
Menan, Pierre
    Mangin, Marie Louise   1-28-176X
Metai, Joseph
    Guelle, Marie   11-8-1813
Metayer, Louis Levron dit
    Marieva (Piankickias indian)   7-10-1787
Miezet, Marie Louise
    Goyau, Antoine   11-27-1830
Millet dit La Tremouille, Jacque
    Tartre, Julie   2-14-1771
Millet, John Baptiste
    Perodeau, Angelique   2-26-1775
Millet, Rosalie
    Barsalou, Jean Baptiste   8-20-1798
Millot, Felicite
    Brossard, Joseph   2-23-1789
Mizot,   (bride)
    Bono, Auguste   4-6-1795
Moise, Jean Baptiste
    Grimard, Geneieve   7-6-1795
Mominy, Jean
    Ravalette, Marguerite   8-16-1802
Montplaiser, Andre
   Cardinal, Jeanne (widow of Jean Baptiste Tougas) 4-10-179X
Moyse, Charles
    Bayarion, Francoise   5-23-1796
Moyse, Jean Baptiste (widower of Geneieve Grimard)
   Cournouillier, Geneieve (widow of Pierre Latour) 10-1-1810
Moyse, Susanne
    Dubois, Charles   6-16-1828
Munier, Jean
    Vaudry, Angelique   11-4-1793
Meau ? Suzanne (falsely called Therese)see: Fausement
    Toulon dit Canichen, Jean   12-30-1788

Noval, Hypolithe
    Delisle, Cecile   5-28-1808
Noyan, Louis
   Racine, Angelique (widow of Pierre Cornouailler 7-27-1795
Noyse, Joseph
    Deboise, Jeannette   1-19-1829

O'Neille, Joseph
    Delisle, Victoire   12-25-1809
Ouellet, Agatha or Agate (widow of Pierre De Mers)
    Paquin, Francois   5-7-1787
Ouellet, John Baptiste (widower of Geneieve Guibord)
    Colon, Geneieve (widow of Pierre Grimard)   9-14-1785
Ouillette, Agate or Agatha
    De Mers or Dumais, Pierre   2-25-1775
Oise, Michel
    Du Devoir, Barbe   8-23-1763
Outlas, Francoise (widow of Antoine Droit De Richarville)
    Dagenay, Ambroise   1-21-1773

Pacanne, Marie
    Bonneau, Jean Baptiste   11-6-1786
Page, Dominique
    Bayargeon, Pelagie   11-29-1828
Page, Guillaume
    Schabarte, Josepte   2-26-1770
Page, Guillaume
    Huneau, Marie Victory (widow of Antoine Villeray)   7-26-1778
Page, Josette (widow of Joseph Lamothe)
    Tremblai, Etienne   5-14-1798
Page, Madeleine
    Desjardins, Hiacynthe   1-24-1803
Page, Marie
    Gonzales, Simon   2-27-1798
Page, Marie
    Cournoyer, Pierre   7-13-1829
Pagix, Marie Josephe
    Lamote, Joseph
Paille, Joseph
    Lamoureux, Magdeleine St. Germain   3-19-1770
Paquin, Francois
    Ouellet, Agatha (widow of Pierre De Mers)   5-7-1786
Pelletier, Pierre
    Cardinal, Barbe   7-15-1805
Pellu, Marie Amable
    Denoyan, Jean Louis   1-19-1761
Peltur, Andre
    La Coste, Angelique   1-18-1773
Perodeau, Angelique
    Millet, John Baptiste   2-26-1775
Perodot, Barbe
    Berton dit St. Martin, Jean Baptiste   4-28-1788
Perron, Geneieve (widow of Jean Poteven)
    Chartier, Joseph (widower of Charlotte Renaud) 1-26-1803
Perron, Jeanne
    Desrochers, Joseph   2-27-1770
Perron, Marie
    Chatagny, Ignace   3-19-1790
Perron, Pierre
    Roufiance dit La Violette, Marie Therese   1-26-1773

Perrot, Nicolas
    Edeline, Marie Josepte   7-24-1778
Perthius, Louise
    Crepaux, Louis   11-26-1749
Perthius, Pierre
    Vital, Angelique   1-3-1757
Pethier, Catherine (widow Beket)
    Alard, Louis   9-20-1784
Petit dit La Lumiere, Antoine
    De Villers, Marie Joseph   2-29-1787
Picardand, Alexis
    Bisaillon, Francoise Berenice   3-2-1827
Pinsoneau, Etienne
    Villeneuve, Rose   9-29-1794
Plisson, Francoise (widow of Jean Baptiste Demers)
    Baillargeons, Nicolas?   7-24-1778
Poineau, Marie Anne
    Laviolette, Louis Roussian dit   2-4-1788
Poirer, Marie Josephe (widow of Dominique Bergan)
    Guitard, Pierre Dion dit (widower of Marie Monique Morant)
                                                      2-26-1788
Poirer, Paul
    Raimond, Marie Josephe (widow of _____Tremble) 11-4-1794
Poirier, dit Deleg, Pierre
    Bissonet, Marie (widow of Toussaint De Noyon) 10-17-1785
Poitevin, dit Arpin, Francois
    Chartier, Geneieve   6-2-1794
Poterin, Catherine
    St. Germain, Louis   10-8-1810
Potevin, Joseph
    Caron, Marie   7-22-1828
Potevin, Marie
    Cayon, Francois   7-24-1797
Poudret, Marie Anne
    Amelin, Joseph   1-25-1773
Preville dit Codenoir, Louis
    Mallet, Theresa   5-8-1786

Quere, Pierre
    Antara, Marie Joseph   10-17-1763
Querre see also: Kerry
Querre or Kerry, Elizabeth
    Cardinal, Joseph   10-19-1829
Querre, Geneieve
    Mallet, Louis   5-23-1808
Querre, Therese
    Villencuve, Charles   3-3-1800
Querry, Antoine
    Frederick, Catherine   1-2-1824

Racine, Andre
    Chabot, Cecile   5-21-1793

Racine, Angelique (widow of Pierre Cornouailler)
    Noyon, Louis   7-27-1795

Racine dit St. Marie, Celeste
    Valle, Francois   10-8-1803

Racine dit St. Marie, Francois
    Compagnot, Marie Anne   11-15-1787

Racine, Francois
    Delaurier, Adelaide   7-26-1824

Racine, Francois
    Huberd, Angelique   7-27-1829

Racine dit St. Marie, Henri
    Tougas, Eleanor   8-18-1825

Racine, Jean Baptiste
    Du Devoir, Anne   11-23-1756

Racine dit St. Marie, Marie Louise
    Raimbault, Pierre   7-27-1779

Racine, Marie Louise
    St. Marie, Joseph   5-22-1785

Racine, Marie Therese
    Veilleneuve, Joseph   9-20-1802

Raimbault, Pierre
    Racine St. Marie, Marie Louise   7-27-1779

Raimond, Marie Joseph (widow of _____ Tremble)
    Poirer, Paul   11-4-1794

Rascicot, Elizabeth
    Tremble, Michel   2-12-1827

Rascicot, Francoise
    Caillou, Amable   2-16-1828 ? 1829

Rasicot, Francois
    Compagnot, Francoise   1-23-1800

Ravalet, Louis
    Fevel, Josephte   8-2-1784

Ravalet, Louis
    Campeau, Helene   10-1-1810

Ravalet, Therese
    Renau dit Delaurier, Pierre   11-11-1813

Ravalette, Madeleine
    De Ganne, Joseph   11-29-1790

Ravalette, Marguerite
    Moming, Jean   8-16-1802

Rejembald dit Jerome, Antoine
    Desbiens, Helene   7-19-1828

Rejimbald, Helene
    Compagnotte, Pierre   6-20-1830

Renau see: also Delaurier

Renau dit Delaurier, Pierre
    Ravalet, Therese   11-11-1813

Renaud see: also Desloriez

Renaud dit Desloriez, Desanges (bride)
    Touga, Guillaume   7-6-1801

Ranaud dit Desloriez, Eleanor
    Touga, Auguste   7-6-1801

Renaud dit Desloriez, Geneieve
    Edeline, Francois Xavier Joseph   2-18-1799

Renaud, Thersa
    Chabot, Bernard   5-15-1808

Renault, Charlotte
    Chartier dit Binaque, Joseph (widower of Marie Louise Girardo)
        10-20-1793

Renault, Jean Baptiste
    Mallet, Therese   10-27-1750

Renault, Jean Baptiste
    Bordeleau, Marie Madeline   7-9-1779

Rene, Joseph
    Daher, Elizabeth   5-23-1808

Rene, Joseph Gabriel
    Dagenay, Victoria   6-13-1803

Rene, Louis
    Villeneuvem Marguerite (widow of Antoine Richaville)   7-14-1805

Richard, Agnes
    Vaudry, Jean Baptiste   8-28-1756

Richard, Jean Baptiste
    Mallet, Elizabeth   2-27-1786

Richarville, Antoine Drouet De
    Villeneuve, Marguerite   1-19-1801

Richarville, Antoine Derouet dit
    Cournoyer, Clemente   5-31-1830

Richarville, Marie
    Brouillet, Michel   9-21-1811

Richerville, Sr Antoine Drouet De
    Vaudrie, Marie   7-14-1779

Richerville, Marguerite Drouet De
    Gamelin, Sr Paul   6-6-1785

Riendean, Joachim
    Roussian, Therese (widow of Pierre Perron)   11-17-1787

Rochard, Helene
    Desbiens, Andre   1-24-1803

Rolland, Jacques
    Toiniche, Agathe   2-8-1798

Rolus, Samuel
    Campeau, Jeanne   10-1-1810

Roufiance dit La Violette, Marie Therese
    Perron, Pierre   1-26-1773

Roussian dit La Violette, Louis
    Poineau, Marie Anne   2-4-1788

Roussian, Therse (widow of Pierre Perron)
    Riendeau, Joachim   11-17-1787

Roux, Emanuel
    Coulter, Elene   9-5-1825

Roux, Pierre
    Mallet, Angelique   1-20-1794

Russel, Robert Woodburn
    Cartier - Kirky, Susanne (widoe of Lalumeers)   9-12-1823

Sans Soucison or Sans Souce, Joseph
    Baliarjion, Archeange   10-1-1810

Sanson, Alexander
    Bordeleau, Archange   10-3-1785

Schabert, Josepte
   Page, Guillaume   2-26-1770
Seguien, Agathe
   Chapart, Ambroise
Seguien, Barbe
   Boyer, Francois   5-17-1808
Sequin, dit La Deroute, Barbe
   Boye, Francois   4-24-1792
Sequein, Cecile
   Desnaux, Rene   2-10-1800
Sevigny, Eustache
   Des Noyons, Marguerite   4-27-1806
Soudriette, Charles
   Cardinal, Felicite (widow of Francois Trotier) 10-1-1810
St. Antoine, Francois Vachet dit
   Cardinal, Therse   5-2-1785
St. Antoine, Therese
   Dupre, Louis   2-16-1801
St. Aubin, Claude
   La Feuillade, Marianne (widow of Louis Bergeron) 7-17-1797
St. Aubin, Jean Baptiste
   Denie, Marie Louise   10-19-1760
St. Aubin, Louis
   Bergan, Catharine   4-16-1787
St. Germain, Felicity
   Codere, Rene   2-13-1786
St. Germain, Louis
   Poterin, Catherine   10-8-1810
St. Germain Lamoureux, Magdeleine
   Paille, Joseph   3-19-1770
St. Jean, Nicholas Tirard dit
   Tirio, Marie Ann   11-17-1787
St. Marie, Celeste Racene dit
   Valle, Francois   10-8-1803
St. Marie, Henri
   Dubois, Barbe   2-12-1827 license
St. Marie, Henri Racine dit
   Tougas, Eleanor   8-18-1828
St. Marie, Joseph
   Racine, Marie Louise   5-22-1785
St. Martin, Jean Baptiste Berton dit
   Perodot, Barbe   4-28-1788

Tartre, Julie
   Millet dit La Tremouille, Jacque   2-14-1771
Tesie or Texier, Francois
   La Fontaine, Catherine   6-29-1795
Tetro, Jean Baptiste
   Clermont, Marie Louise (widow of Guillaume Deperon) 11-28-1787
Texier or Tesie, Francois
   La Fontaine, Catherine   6-29-1795

Theriaque, Michel
    Andre, Therese   1-7-1796
Thierie, Marie Joseph La Tulippe dit
    Lefevre, Antoine   1-21-1788
Tirard dit St. Jean, Nicholas
    Tirio, Marie Anne   11-17-1787
Tiracque, Jacques
    Mallet, Marguerite   11-3-1829
Tiriaque, Joseph
    Villeneuve, Helene   5-1-1827
Tirio, Marie Anne
    Tirard dit St. Jean, Nicholas   11-17-1787
Toiniche, Agathe
    Rolland, Jacques   2-8-1798
Touga, Alexander
    Boyer, Marie Louise   8-21-1826 license
Touga, Auguste
    Deloriez, Eleanor Renaud dit   7-6-1801
Touga, Francois
    Valle, Geneieve   7-15-1805
Touga, Guillaume (groom)
    Renaud dit Desloriez, Desange   7-6-1801
Touga, Joseph
    Cardinal, Marie Jeanne   1-16-1773
Touga, Jsoeph
    Valle, Francoise   4-22-1801
Tougas, Auguste
    Laplante, Julie   1-4-1830
Tougas, Eleanor
    Racine dit St. Marie, Henri   8-18-1828
Tougas, Francoise
    Querre, Antoine   6-30-1828
Tougas, Guillaume
    Barrios, Angelique   8-7-1826
Tougas, Jean Baptiste
    Crepeau, Catherine   1-18-1773
Tougas, Susanne
    Bonhomme, J. Baptiste   1-4-1830
Tougas, Susanne
    Kerry, John B. (Cary)   5-31-1830
Toulon dit Canichen, Jean
    Neau?, Suzanne (Therese)   12-30-1788
Toulon dit Genichon, Marie
    Chartier, Jean Baptiste Benae dit   11-8-1813
Touya   see: Touga
Trampe or Trempe dit Cornouailler, Victoire
    Dejean, Phillipe   7-21-1794
Tremblai, Archange
    Boucher, Joseph   6-13-1814
Tremblai, Etienne
    Page, Josette (widow of Joseph Lamothe)   5-14-1798
Tremble, Michel
    Rascicot, Elizabeth   2-12-1827

Tremont, Jean
    Meenis - Mares, Joseph Polly (widow of Jean Meenis) 8-22-1801
Trempe see: Trampe
Trottier, Francois
    Cardinal, Marie Felicite   1-2-1792
Turpen, Rose
    Grimard, Charles   12-19-1809
Turpen, Francois
    Guelle, Josephine   7-16-1805
Turpen, Louis
    Cartier, Celeste   5-24-1830
Vachet dit St. Antoine, Francois
    Cardinal, Therese   5-2-1785
Vachet, Francois
    D'eneau, Francoise   5-30-1808
Valeix, Alexander (widower of Francoise Boneau)
    Gaudere, Felicite   5-23-1793
Valique, Francis
    Berthiaume, Angelique   8-2-1784
Valle, Alexander
    Boneau, Frances   8-2-1874
Valle, Alexandre
    Langlois, Jannete   10-26-1795
Valle, Francois
    Racine dit St. Marie, Celeste   10-8-1803
Valle, Francoise
    Touga, Joseph   4-22-1801
Valle, Geneieve
    Touga, Francois   7-15-1805
Valle, Pelagie
    Baillargeon, Nicolas   5-23-1808
Valle, Rayait - Raphael
    Grimard, Marie   1-4-1830
Vaudrie, John Baptiste
    Chapart, Marie Claire   6-20-1785
Vaudrie, Marie
    Richerville, Antoine Drouet De   7-14-1779
Vaudry, Angelique
    Munier, Jean   11-4-1793
Vaudry, Jean Baptiste
    Richard, Agnes   8-28-1756
Vaudry, Ursule
    Gamelin, Pierre   7-24-1778
Veillencuvem, Joseph
    Racine, Marie Therese   9-20-1802
Villeneuve, Charles
    Bonneau, Geneieve   1-14-1773
Villeneuve, Charles
    Querre, Therese   3-3-1800
Villeneuve, Felicite
    Gaudere, Alexis   9-22-1829
Villeneuve, Francoise
    Gamelin or Gamenen, Pierre   11-11-1813

Villeneuve, Genevieve
    Bonhomme, Jean Baptiste   4-15-1793
Villeneuve, Helene
    Tiriaque, Joseph   5-1-1827
Villeneuve, Marguerite
    Richarville, Antoine Drouet De   1-19-1801
Villeneuve, Marguerite (widow of Antoine Richarville)
    Rene, Louis   7-14-1805
Villeneuve, Marie
    Dalbe, Antoine   7-30-1826
Villeneuve, Rose
    Pinsoneau, Etienne   9-29-1794
Vital, Angelique
    Perthuis, Pierre   1-3-1757

DECEASED SPOUSES

Bazinet, Francois
   see: Bonneau, Angelique
Beket, _____
   see: Pethier, Catherine
Bergan, Dominique
   see: Poirier, Marie Joseph
Bergeron, Louis
   See: La Feuillade, Marianne
Boneau, Francoise
   See: Valeix, Alexandre
Brouillet, Barbe
   See: Baron, Joseph

Cardinal, Nicholas
   See: Gerard, Marie Joseph
Cornouailler, Pierre
   See: Racine, Angelique

Danis, Marie Louise
   See: Barrois, Lambert
Daperon, Guillaume
   See: Clermont, Marie Louise
DeComte, _____
   See: Clermont, Ursule
Demers, Jean Bte
   See: Plisson, Francoise
De Mers, Pierre
   See: Ouellet, Agathe or Agate
De Noyon, Toussaint
   See: Bissonet, Marie
Deperon, Guillaume
   See: Clermont, Marie Louise

Fueillade, Joseph De La
   See: Emelin, Marianne

Gamelin, Catherine
   See: Gamelin, Antoine
Gamelin, Dame Marie Jane
   See: Le Gras, John Marie
Ganichon, Jean Toulon dit
   See: Fausement?, Susan Therese
Garardo, Marie Louise
   See: Chartier dit Benague, Joseph
Girardo, Marie Louise
   See: Binaque, Joseph Chartier dit
Girould, Laurent
   See: Brouillet, Barbe
Girourd, Laurent
   See: Brouillet, Barbe
Grimard, Geneieve
   See: Moyse, Jean Baptiste
Grimard, Pierre
   See: Colon, Geneieve
Guibord, Geneieve
   See: Oullet, John

Lamothe, Joseph
   See: Page, Josette
Latour, Pierre
   See: Cournouiller, Geneieve
Latulipe, Pierre Querie dit
   See: Bono, Angelique
Lalumiere, _____
   See: Cartier, Sisanne
Lefebvre, Sr Charles
   See: Desvegnets, Dame Maris
Levron, Joseph
   See: Cardinal, Celeste
Levron dit Mitteller, _____
   See: Custos, Marie

Marie, Antoine
   See: Chicamicqe, Marie Anne
Meenis, John
   See: Meenis, Marie Joseph Polly
Mitteller, _____ Leveron dit
   See: Custos, Marie
Morant, Marie Monique
   See: Dion dit Guitard, Pierre

Perron, Pierre
   See: Roussian, Therese
Potevin, Jean
   See: Perron, Geneieve

Querie dit Latulipe, Pierre
    See: Bono, Angelique

Renault, Charlotte
    See: Cartier, Joseph
Richarville, Antoine Drout De
    See: Outlas, Francoise
Richarville, Antoine
    See: Villeneuve, Marguerite

St. Aubin, _____
    See: La Feuillade, Marianne

Touga, Jean Baptiste
    See: Cardinal, Jeanne
Toulon dit Ganichon, Jean
    See: Fausement?, Susan Therese
Tremble,_____
    See: Raimond, Marie Josephe
Trotier, Francois
    See: Cardinal, Felicite

Villeneuve, Charles
    See: Bonneau, Geneieve
Villeray, Antoine
    See: Huneau, Marie Victoire

Wiron, Marie
    See: Babini, Michel Ange

ST FRANCIS XAVIER CATHOLIC CHURCH

VINCENNES, IND.

MARRIAGE RECORDS

1814 - 1838

PART II

BY

BARBARA SCHULL WOLFE

25 March 1987

Typed by: Rosalie Looker Rowe

Alarie, Cecile (Delaurier)
    Mallet, Francois   no date #320   (8-14-1817)
Amelin, _____ (Madame)
    Drouillard,_____ (Mr)   no date # 320
Amelin, Francoise
    Desjean, Antoine (Dejean)   10-7-1827 civil (12-4-1826)
Andre, Amable
    Daniel, Elizabeth   5-2-1831
Andre, Amable
    Boucher, Marie Louise   1-18-1837
Andre, Elizabeth
    Villeneuve, Charles   5-29-1835
Andre, Josephine
    Barrois, Joseph   3-8-1834 remarried
Andre, Mary Anne
    Stout, James   8-14-1834
Andre, Pierre
    Bonhomme, Barbe   10-7-1827 civil (2-20-1815)
Andre, Pierre
    Compagnot, Elizabeth   11-16-1835
Andre, Joseph
    Valle, Catherine   8-18-1823

Bailey, Elizabeth
    Lognon, Francios   1-2-1838
Bailes, Hester
    Laugel, Peter   12-31-1838
Baillargeon, Victoire
    Cartier, Inadore   4-25-1820
Barbau, Francoise
    Girardin, Jean Bte   5-31-1831
Barbot, Jean Bte
    Mallet, Marie Anne   4-23-1838
Barnabe, Antoine
    Laviolette, Marie   10-7-1827 civil (8-8-1825
Barrois, J. (Joseph) M. Jr
    Gamelin, Adelaide (Marie Joseph) no date #320 (8-4-1807)
Barrois, Joseph
    Andre, Josephine   3-8-1834 remarried
Barrois, Toussaint
    Bonhomme, Jeanne   1-6-1834
Barron, Joseph
    Brouillette, Marianne   8-13-1835
Barsalou, Marie
    Letour, Pierre   (married 11 Mos.)   6-26-1823
Bay, Sophia
    Muckensturn, Anthony   7-26-1838
Bayard, John Francois
    Bonneau, Marie Anne   7-7-1823
Bayargeon - Baillargeon, Francoise
    Bouche, Vital   4-24-1832
Beauregard, Antoine
    Querry, Geneieve   10-27-1818

Beckman, Catherine
    Dustenberg, Gerhard Heinrick   12-27-1837
Beckus, Ann
    Hays, William   6-23-1834
Benagne, Therese
    Mete, Charles   6-6-1836
Bohm, Charles Louis
    Wilhelm, Catherine   10-7-1838
Bonhomme, Barbe
    Andre, Pierre   10-7-1827 civil   (2-20-1815)
Bonhomme, Charles
    Levron, Veronique   11-30-1835
Bonhomme, Geneieve
    Hunot, Joseph   11-23-1818
Bonhomme, Jeanne
    Barrois, Toussaint   1-6-1834
Bonhomme, Marie Anne
    Richarville, Jean Baptiste 10-7-1827 civil (11-4-1825)
Bonhomme, Michel
    Delorier, Marie   10-9-1835
Bonneau, Marie Ann
    Bayard, John Francois   7-7-1823
Bonneau, Susanne
    Soudrier, Francois   1-30-1837
Bono, Francios
    Ravalet, Francoise   5-16-1816 remarried
Bono, Jeanne
    Souligny, Joseph   1-21-1833
Bordeleau, Pierre
    Poitdevin, Julie   10-7-1827
Bordeleau, Suzanne
    Campot, Antoine   1-10-1820
Bouche, Celeste
    Genereux, Francois   5-21-1832
Bouche, Vital
    Bayargeon - Baillargeon, Francoise   4-24-1832
Boucher, Baptiste
    Racicot, Marie   2-3-1818
Boucher, Felix
    Richardville, Celeste Drouet de   8-13-1838
Boucher, Francois
    Dequinte, Marie   9-19-1820
Boucher, Marie
    Richarville, Henri   10-7-1827 civil (8-7-1822)
Boucher, Marie Louise
    Andre, Amable   1-18-1837
Boucher, (Mary) maiden name not stated(widow of Joseph Boucher)
    Cardinal, Medard   10-7-1827 civil (1-2-1826)
Boucher, Suzanne
    Richardville, Michel Frouet de   2-3-1818
Boucher, Vital
    Vallet, Marie   5-18-1816 remarried
Boucher, Vital
    Chabot, Ursule (Lawrence Co. Ill.) 10-7-1827 (civil 5-28-1827)

Boyer, Barbe
    Grimard, Jean Bpt   10-7-1827   (civil 5-23-1827)
Boyer, Francois
    Compagnot, Marie Thomas   7-14-1823
Boyer, Francois
    Sequin dit Laderoute, Marie Anne   2-12-1838
Boyer, Louis
    Mete (Mattey), Catherine   5-16-1816 remarried
Boyer, Susanne
    Richardville, Pierre Drouet de   12-27-1837
Brouillette, Marianne
    Barron, Joseph   8-13-1835
Brouillette, Pierre
    Compo, Victoire   2-18-1833
Brown, Catherine A.
    Farrell, Edward (Jefferson Co. Ind.)   8-27-1837
Brown, Marie
    Sheern, James   4-29-1833

Cabassier, Adelaide
    Ravalette, Antoine   7-6-1818
Cabassier, Marie Louise
    Cartier, Louis   10-7-1827   (civil 12-30-1825)
Cabassier, Pierre
    Ravalette, Elizabeth   6-24-1820
Cabassier, Victoire
    Tessier, Francois   1-10-1820
Campot, Antoine
    Bordeleau, Suzanne   1-10-1820
Cardinal, Denis
    Courtright, Francoise   2-19-1838
Cardinal, Elizabeth
    Primrose, Mordecai   12-15-1837
Cardinal, Francoise
    Cochran, Michel (b. 1799)   6-26-1823
Cardinal, Henrietta (widow of Louis Loyon)
    Paget, Dominique (widower of Pelagie Valey) 6-18-1932
Cardinal, Joseph
    Delaurier, Catherine   7-14-1823
Cardinal, J. (Julienne)
    Languedoc, Charles   5-11-1816 remarried
Cardinal, Medard
    Boucher, (Mary) (widow of Joseph Boucher)10-7-1827(civil 1-2-1826)
Cardinal, Toussaint
    Cornoyer, Helene   1-12-1835
Carretier, Susanne
    Latumiere, Antoine Petit dit   10-19-1818
Cartier, Antoine
    Laforet, Julie   10-7-1827
Cartier, Inadore
    Baillargeon, Victoire   4-25-1820
Cartier, Louis
    Cabassier, Marie Louise   10-7-1827   (civil 12-30-1825)

Cary See: Querry
Cayot See: Kyout
Cayot - Kyout, Louis
    Dupre, Julie   5-11-1834 remarried
Chabot, Francoise
    Goyaunt, Paul   11-27-1834
Charbot, Ursule (Lawerance Co. Ill.)
    Boucher, Vital   10-7-1827   (civil 5-27-1827)
Chapa, Auguste
    Denot, Barbe   10-12-1818
Chappart, Marie Anne (Lefevre)
    Grimard, Charles   1-29-1835
Chenet, Marie
    Denoud, Pierre   5-9-1834 remarried
Cochran, Michel (b. 1799)
    Cardinal, Francoise   6-26-1823
Compagnot, Elizabeth
    Andre, Pierre   11-16-1835
Compagnot, Marie Therese
    Boyer, Francois   7-14-1823
Compagnotte, Francoise (widow of Francois Racicot)
    Valee, Francois   8-18-1832
Compagnotte, Marcellite
    Laplante, Joseph   2-6-1837
Compo, Victoire
    Brouillete, Pierre   2-18-1833
Cornoyer, Helene
    Cardinal, Toussaint   1-12-1835
Coulter, Matilda
    Pitcher, John   12-26-1819
Courtright, Francoise
    Cardinal, Denis   2-19-1838
Craft, George
    (Desrosiers) Richardville, Geneieve   4-26-1834 remarried
Crely, Charles
    Richard, Marguerite   7-6-1818

Dabien, Marie J.
    Hiler, Charles Pierre (of Morris Co.N.J.)   6-10-1835
Dagehet, Mary (part indian)
    Peckhem, Lewis   9-27-1819
Dalbe, Dolby Antoine
    Villeneuve, Marie   10-7-1827   (civil 11-22-1825)
D'albee, Joseph
    Malette, Marie Louise (widow of Charles Cabassier) 3-26-1831
Daniel, Elizabeth
    Andre, Amable   5-2-1831
Dauphin, Jean Bte
    Laforet, Marianne   9-11-1820
Dejean See: Desjean
Dejean - Desjean, Antoine
    Amelin, Francoise   10-7-1827   (civil 12-4-1826)
Dejean, Clorisse
    Sequin dit Laderoute, Louis   11-23-1818

Delaurier, Catherine
    Cardinal, Joseph   7-14-1823
Delaurier - Alarie, Cecil
    Mallet, Francois   no date #320   (civil 8-14-1817
Delauier, Francoise
    Languedoc, Louis   5-11-1816 remarried
Delaurier, Louison
    Lefevre, Henriette   5-26-1817
Deligne, Francoise
    Godaire, Pierre   1-30-1832
Deligne, Geneieve
    Grimard, Jean Bté   5-7-1837
Delile, Marie Jane
    Mallet, Louis   10-16-1837
Delille, Cecile (widow of Paul Monval)
    Edeline, Joseph (widower of Geneieve Deslorier) 2-22-1819
Delille, Josette
    Latour, Henry   6-19-1820
Delisle, Jean Baptiste
    Vallet, Victoire   10-19-1818
Delorier, Marie
    Bonhomme, Michel   10-9-1835
Delorier, Victoire
    Peltier, Jacques   5-30-1833
Deloriers, Francois Xavier
    Racine, Cecile   8-7-1820
Deloriers, Marianne Renaud dit
    Racine, Jean Bpt   7-3-1820
Denot, Barbe
    Chapa, Auguste   10-12-1818
Denoud, Pierre
    Chenet, Marie   5-9-1834 remarried
Dequinte, Marie
    Boucher, Francois   9-19-1820
De Rome, Charles
    Graeter, Marie   6-20-1820
Des Carraux, Francoise Doram dit
    Joyeux, Guillaume   2-14-1820
Desjean See: Dejean
Desjean - Dejean, Antoine
    Amelin, Francoise   10-7-1826   (civil 12-4-1826)
Desjean, Julie
    Richard, Jean Bte   11-1-1819
Deslorier, Marianne
    Mallet, Francois   8-14-1818
Desrosiers, Geneieve (Richardville)
    Craft, George   4-26-1834 remarried
Dielle, Josette (widow of Francois Calpier?)
    Montmenier, Jean (widower of Marguerite Brizard) 9-12-1818
Dolby - Dalby, Antoine
    Villeneuve, Marie   10-7-1827   (civil 11-22-1825)
Dolehun - Dollahan, John
    Lansdown, Elizabeth (widow of Joseph Glover) 1-30-1820

Doram dit Des Carraux, Francoise
    Joyeux, Guillaume   2-14-1820
Dorsey, Ann
    Largan, William (Vernon, Ind.)   8-7-1837
Droiullard, _____ Mr
    Amelin, _____ Madame   no date #320
Dubois, Euphrosyne - Eliza
    Watson, George Hyrum   7-17-1837
Dubois? Sub, Michael
    Languedoc, Francoise   5-10-1816 remarried
Dubois, Pierre
    Monplaiser, Barbe   8-26-1820
Dudevoir, Marie
    Pelletier, Pierre   8-18-1832
Dupre, Julie
    Cayot - Kyout, Louis   5-11-1834 remarried
Dupre, Louis
    Gonzales, Francoise   2-22-1834 remarried
Dusterberg, Gerhard Heinrich
    Beckman, Catherine   12-27-1837

Edeline, Joseph (widower of Geneieve Deslorier)
    Delille, Cecile (widow of Paul Monval)   2-22-1819
Edline, Pierre
    Latour, Marie   4-30-1813

Farrell, Edward
    Brown, Catherine A. (Jefferson Co. Ind.)   8-27-1837
Farrell, Michael (Vernon, Ind.)
    Mac Ginty, Mary   8-7-1837
Fontenac, Joseph Querry (Cary) dit
    White, Mary   11-30-1837
Fontenaque, Michel Querret de
    Tougas, Marcellite   2-6-1837
Fromeier, William
    Myers, Mary   8-18-1838

Gail, Marie
    Grimard, Amable   2-12-1838
Gamelin, Adelaide (Marie Josephe)
    Barrois, J. (Joseph) M. Jr no date #320   (civil 8-4-1807)
Gamelin, Adelaide
    Mallet, Jean Bte   5-21-1838
Gamelin, Elizabeth
    Laplante, Pierre   1-16-1820
Gamelin, Marie
    Mallet, Pierre   8-6-1838
Gautier dit St Germain, Charles
    St Marie, Felicite (Racinw dit) no date #320 (before 1825)
Genereux, Francois
    Bouche, Celeste   5-21-1832

Genereux, Francis
    Peltier, Felice   2-15-1836

Girardin, Jean Bte
    Barbau, Franciose   5-31-1831

Godaire, Pierre
    Deligne, Francoise   1-30-1832

Godaire, Pierre
    Languedoc, Marie Helene   1-30-1837

Godere, Pierre
    Mallet, Geneieve   10-2-1837

Gonzales, Francoise
    Dupre, Louis   2-22-1834 remarried

Goyan, Benoit -Burway
    Lenau, Elizabeth - Marie Louise   10-7-1827 remarried

Goyaut, Paul
    Chabot, Francoise   11-27-1834

Graeter, Marie
    De Rome, Charles   6-20-1820

Grenier, Martial
    Lafond, Barbe   1-31-1834 remarried

Grimard, Amable
    Gail, Marie   2-12-1838

Grimard, Charles
    Chappart, Marie Ann (Lefevre)   1-29-1835

Grimard, Geneieve
    Moyse, Charles   1-7-1819

Grimard, (Jean Bpte)
    Boyer, Barbe   10-7-1827   (5-23-1827 Civil)

Grimard, Jean Bte
    Deligne, Geneieve   5-7-1837

Grimard, Pierre
    Mayer, Toinette   1-18-1836

Gupton, Melany
    Rogers, Patrick (farmer near Pettite Bon-Pas) 4-23-1835

Hayes, William
    Beckus, Ann   6-23-1834

Hiler, Charles Pierre (of Morris Co. N.J.)
    Dabien, Marie J.   6-10-1835

Hinds, John (Madison, Ind.)
    Murdock, Bridget   7-30-1837

Hoopher, Chrisrian
    Spits, Elizabeth   12-5-1833

Huno, Eleanor
    Richarville, Antoine   4-15-1836   (9-2-1844 Validated)

Hunot, Joseph
    Bonhomme, Geneieve   11-23-1818

Hunot, Josette
    Richarville, Jean Bte   2-24-1834 remarried

Hunot, Pelagie
    Troquier, Francois   7-19-1819

Jenkins, George Mary (colored)
    Leveyer, Rosalie (colored)   9-12-1836
Johnston, Robert
    Vachet, Marianne   3-22-1834 remarried
Joyeuse, Francoise
    Reeves, William   6-2-1832
Joyeux, Guillaume
    Doram dit Des Carraux, Francoise   2-14-1820

Kyout See: Cayout
Kyout - Cayout, Louis (of St. Louis)
    Poitdevin, Susanne   5-9-1831
Kyout - Cayout, Louis
    Dupre, Julie   5-11-1834 remarried

La Coste, Charles (married at Riviere a Chat)
    Valle, Marcelline (Wabash Co. Ill.)   1-16-1835
La Coste, Felicite
    Vacher, Pierre   12-31-1838
La Coste, Joseph
    Racuse, Marianne   1-30-1832
La Coste dit Langdo, Julie
    Tougas dit Laviolette, Francois   5-6-1833
Lacroix, Dominique
    Petite dit Laiumiere, Henriette   9-3-1821
Laderout, Louis Sequin dit
    Dejean, Clorisse   11-23-1818
Lafeuillade, Marie
    Mete, Pierre   4-18-1834 remarried
Lafond, Barbe
    Grenier, Martial   1-31-1834 remarried
Lafond, Jean Antoine (widower of cecile Boyer)
    Racine, Barbe   5-30-1819
Lafond, Mary
    Malet, Peter   1-6-1835
Laforet, Julie
    Cartier, Antoine   10-7-1827
Laforet, Marianne
    Dauphin, Jean Bte   9-11-1820
Lalumiere, Henriette Petite dit
    Lacroix, Dominique   9-3-1821
Langdo, Julie Lacoste dit
    Tougas dit Laviolette, Francois   5-6-1833
Languedoc, Charles
    Cardinal, J. (Julienne)   5-11-1816 remarried
Languedoc, Francoise
    (Dubois) Sub, Michael   5-10-1816 remarried
Languedoc, Jean Bte
    Pelletier, Mary Anne   11-26-1837
Languedoc, Louis
    Delaurier, Francoise   5-11-1816 remarried
Languedoc, Marie Helene
    Godaire, Pierre   1-30-1837

Lansdown, Elizabeth (widow of Joseph Glover)
    Dolehun - Dollahan, John   1-30-1820
Laplante, Elizabeth
    Stewart, James   7-13-1823   4-16-1834 license
Laplante, Helene (Ill.)
    Wire, John Patterson (Ky.)   1-17-1835
Laplante, Joseph
    Compagnotte, Marcellite   2-6-1837
Laplante, Pierre
    Gamelin, Elizabeth   1-16-1820
Largan, William (Vernon, Ind.)
    Dorsey, Ann   8-7-1837
Latour, Augustin
    Laviolette dit Violon, Marguerite   1-25-1819
Latour, Henry
    Delille, Josette   6-19-1820
Latour, Jean Bte
    Sezan, Henriette   5-26-1817
Latour, Marie
    Edline, Pierre   4-30-1813
Latumiere, Antoine Petit dit
    Carretier, Susanne   10-19-1818
Laugel, Peter
    Bailes, Hester   12-31-1838
Laviolette, Francois Tougas dit
    Lacoste dit Langdo, Julie   5-6-1833
Laviolette, Magdeleine
    Troquier, Paul   1-31-1834 remarried
Laviolette dit Violon, Marguerite
    Latour, Augustin   1-25-1819
Laviolette, Marie
    Barnabe, Antoine   10-7-1827   8-8-1825 civil
Lefevre, Henriette
    Delaurier, Louison   5-26-1817
Lefevre - Chappart, Marie Ann
    Grimard, Charles   1-29-1835
Lenau, Elizabeth - Marie Louise
    Goyau, Benoit - Burway   10-7-1827   8-24-1826 civil
Letour, Pierre
    Barsalou, Marie   (married 11 Mos.)   6-26-1823
Leveyer, Rosalie (colored)
    Jenkins, George Mary (colored)   9-12-1836
Levron, Veronique
    Bonhomme, Charles   11-30-1835
Lognion, Susanne
    Racico, Sylvester   9-3-1832
Lognon, Francois
    Bailey, Elizabeth   1-2-1838
Lognon, Marie
    Racico, Antoine   1-23-1832

McDonald, May Ann
    Osborn, Jonathan   8-13-1835

Mac Ginty, Mary
    Farrell, Michael (Vernon, Ind.)   8-7-1837

Mahoney, Nancy
    Thomas, Henry   (no other date given)   1833
Malet, Peter
    Lafond, Mary   1-6-1835
Malette, Marie Louise   (widow of Charles Cabassier)
    D'Alvee, Joseph   3-26-1831
Mallet, Francois
    Alarie - Delaurier, Cecile (nodate #320)   8-14-1817 Civil
Mallet, Francois
    Deslorier, Marianne   8-14-1818
Mallet, Geneieve
    Godere, Pierre   10-2-1837
Mallet, Jean Bte
    Gamelin, Adelaide   5-21-1833
Mallet, Louis
    Delile, Marie Jane   10-16-1837
Mallet, Marie Anne
    Barbot, Jean Bte   4-23-1838
Mallet, Pierre
    Gamelin, Marie   8-6-1838
Mallette, Virginia
    Turpin, Charles   4-8-1833
Mayer, Toinette
    Grimard, Pierre   1-18-1836
Mete - Mattey, Catherine
    Boyer, Louis   5-16-1816 remarried
Mete, Charles
    Benagne, Therese   6-6-1836
Mete, Magdeleine
    Mondou, Martial   5-7-1821
Mete, Piere
    Lafeuillade, Marie   4-18-1834 remarried
Meti, Pierre
    Ravalette, Marie   10-2-1820
Momeni, Antoine
    Steward, Marie   1-13-1834
Momenil, Joseph
    Richarville, Marie Drouet de   1-7-1833
Mondou, Martial
    Mete, Magdeleine   5-7-1821
Monplaisir, Barbe
    Dubois, Pierre   8-26-1820
Montmenier, Jean (widower of Marguerite Brizard)
    Dielle, Josette (widow of Francois Calpier)   9-12-1818
Moyse, Charles
    Grimard, Geneieve   1-7-1819
Moyse, Marie Ann (married at Riviere Au Chat)
    Tougas, Francois   1-17-1835
Muckensturn, Anthony
    Bay, Sophia   7-26-1838

Murdock, Bridget
    Hinds, John   (Madison, Ind.) 7-30-1837
Myers, Mary
    Fromeier, William 8-18-1838

Osborn, Jonathan
    McDonald, Mary Ann 8-13-1835

Paget, Dominique (widower of Pelagie Valey)
    Cardinal, Henrietta (widow of Louis Logon) 6-18-183X
Peckhem, Lewis
    Dagehet, Mary   (part indian) 9-27-1819
Pelletier, Mary Anne
    Languedoc, Jean Bte 11-26-1837
Pelletier, Pierre
    Dudevoir, Marie 8-18-1832
Peltier, Felice
    Genereux, Francis 2-15-1836
Peltier, Jacques
    Delorier, Victoire 5-30-1833
Petite dit Lalumiere, Antoine
    Carreitier, Susanne 10-19-1818
Petite dit Lalumiere, Helenore
    Picard, Alexis 10-23-1820
Petite dit Lalumiere, Henriette
    Lacroix, Dominique 9-3-1821
Picard, Alexis
    Petite dit Lalumiere, Helenore 10-23-1820
Pitcher, John
    Coulter, Matilda 12-26-1819
Picher, Joseph
    Spits, Catherine 11-16-1835
Poidevin, Francois
    Sanson, Victoire 7-6-1818
Poitdevin, Julie
    Bordeleau, Pierre 10-7-1827
Poitdevin, Susanne
    Kyout - Cayot, Louis 5-9-1831
Primrose, Mordicai
    Cardinal, Elizabeth 12-5-1837

Querrey, Geneieve
    Beauregard, Antoine 10-27-1818
Querrie, Geneieve (widow of Louis Mallet)
    Godaire, Francois (widower of Marie Bono) 12-27-1832
Querry (Cary) dit Fontenac, Joseph
    White, Mary 11-30-1837
Querret de Fontenaque, Michel
    Tougas, Marcellite 2-6-1837

Racico, Antoine
    Lognon, Marie   1-23-1832
Racico, Sylvester
    Lognion, Susanne   9-3-1832
Racicot, Marie
    Boucher, Baptiste   2-3-1818
Racine, Barbe
    Lafond, Jean Antoine (widower of Cecile Boyer) 5-30-1819
Racine, Cecile
    Deloriers, Francois Xavier   8-7-1820
Racine dit St. Marie, Felicite
    Gautier dit St. Germain, Charles (no date #320) before 1825
Racine, Jean Bte
    Renaud, dit Deloriers, Marianne   7-3-1820
Racuse, Marianne
    Lacoste, Joseph   1-30-1832
Ravalet, Francois
    Tremblay, Angelique   1-23-1837
Ravalet, Francoise
    Bono, Francois   5-16-1816 remarried
Ravalette, Antoine
    Cabassier, Adelaide   7-6-1818
Ravalette, Elizabeth
    Cabassier, Pierre   6-24-1820
Ravalette, Marie
    Meti, Pierre   10-2-1820
Reeves, William
    Joyeuse, Francoise   6-2-1832
Ranaud dit Delorier, Marianne
    Racine, Jean Baptiste   7-3-1820
Richard, Jean Bte
    Desjean, Julie   11-1-1819
Richard, Marguerite
    Crely, Charles   7-6-1818
Richarville, Antoine
    Huno, Eleanor   4-15-1836   (-2-1844 validated
Richardville, Celeste Drouet de
    Boucher, Felix   8-13-1838
Richardville, Genevieve Desrosiers
    Craft, George   4-16-1834 remarried
Richarville, Henri (Drouet)
    Boucher, Marie   10-7-1827   8-7-1822 Civil
Richarville, Jean Baptiste
    Bonhomme, Marie Ann   10-7-1827   11-4-1825 Civil
Richarville, Jean Baptiste
    Hunot, Josette   2-24-1834 remarried
Richarville, Marie Drouet de
    Momenil, Joseph   1-7-1833
Richardville, Michel Drouet de
    Boucher, Suzanne   2-3-1818
Richardville, Pierre Drouet de
    Boyer, Susanne   12-27-1837
Roger, Patrick (farmer near Petite Bon-Pas)
    Gupton, Melany   4-23-1835

St. Germain, Charles   (Gautier dit)
    St. Marie, Felicite (Racine dit) no date #320-- before 1825
St. Marie, Felicite (Racine dit)
    St. Germain, Charles (Gautier dit) no date #320--before 1825
Sanson, Victoire
    Poidevin, Francois   7-6-1818
Sequin dit Laderout, Louis
    Dejean Clorisse   11-23-1818
Sequin dit Ladiroute, Marie Anne
    Boyer, Francois   2-12-1838
Sezan, Henriette
    Latour, Jean Bte   5-26-1817
Sheern, James
    Brown, Marie   4-29-1833
Soudrier, Francois
    Bonneau, Susanne   1-30-1837
Souligny, Joseph
    Bono, Jeanne   1-21-1833
Spits, Catherine
    Picher, Joseph   11-16-1835
Spits, Elizabeth
    Hoopher, Christian   12-5-1833
Stewart, James
    Laplante, Elizabeth   7-13-1823-license- 4-16-1814 Civil
Stewart, Marie
    Momeni, Antoine   1-13-1834
Stewart, Adele
    Wathen, Edward   10-17-1837
Stout, James
    Andre, Mary Ann   8-14-1834
Sub (Dubois), Michel
    Languedoc, Francoise   5-10-1816 remarried

Tessier, Francois
    Cabassier, Victoire   1-10-1820
Thomas, Henry
    Mahoney, Nancy   (on other date given)   1833
Tougas dit Laviolette, Francois
    Lacoste dit Langdo, Julie   5-6-1833
Tougas, Francois   (married at Riviere Au Chat)
    Moyse, Marie Ann   1-17-1835
Tougas, Marcellite
    Querret de Fontenaque, Michel   2-6-1837
Tremblay, Angelique
    Ravalet, Francois   1-23-1837
Troquier, Francois
    Hunot, Pelagie   7-19-1819
Troquier, Paul
    Laviolette, Magdeleine   1-31-1834 remarried
Turpin, Charles
    Mallette, Virginia   4-8-1833

Vacher, Pierre
    Lacoste, Felicite   12-31-1838

Vachet, Marianne
    Johnston, Robert   3-22-1834 remarried

Valee, Francois
    Compalnotte, Francoise (widow of Francois Racicot) 8-18-1832

Valle, Catherine
    Andre, Joseph   8-18-1823

Vallee, Marcelline (m. at Riviere Au Chat)
    Lacoste, Charles   (Wabash Co. Ill.)   1-16-1835

Vallet, Marie
    Boucher, Vital   5-18-1816 remarried

Vallet, Victoire
    Delisle, Jean Baptiste   10-19-1818

Villeneuve, Charles
    Andre, Elizabeth   5-29-1835

Villeneuve, Marie
    Dalve or Dolby, Antoine   10-7-1827   11-22-1825 Civil

Violon, Marguerite Laviolette dit
    Latour, Augustin   1-25-1819

Wathen, Edward
    Stewart, Adele   10-17-1837

Watson, George Hyrum
    Dubois, Euphrosyne Eliza   7-17-1837

White, Mary
    Querry (Cary) dit Fontenac, Joseph   11-30-1837

Wilhelm, Catherine
    Bohm, Charles Louis   10-7-1838

Wire, John Patterson (Ky.)
    Laplante, Helene (Ill.)   1-17-1835

DECEASED SPOUSES

Bono, Marie
    Godaire, Francois
Boucher, Joseph
    Boucher, (Mary)
Boyer, Cecile
    Lafond, Jean Antoine
Brizard, Marguerite
    Montmemier, Jean

Cabassier, Charles
    Malette, Marie Louise
Calpier, Francois
    Dielle, Josette

Deslorier, Geneieve
    Edeline, Joseph

Glover, Joseph
    Lansdown, Eliazbeth

Lognon, Louis
    Cardinal, Henrietta

Mallet, Louis
    Querrie, Geneieve
Monval, Paul
    Delelle, Cecile

Racicot, Francois
    Compagnotte, Francoise

Valey, Pelagie
    Paget, Dominique

CROSS REFERANCE OF NAMES

Alarie	Delaurier
Arpin	Poitevin, Harpin
Baillargeon	Bayargeon, Bezaillon, Bisaillon
Benac	Benae, Benas, Binaque, Chartier
Berton	St Martin
Canichen	Genichon, Tougas
Cary	Qierry, Kerry
Cayot	Kyout
Chapart	Schabert
Chartier	Benac, Benae, Benas, Binaque
Codenour	Preville
Cornouiller	Cornoyer, Cournouiller, Trempe
De Fontenas	Querrie, Tierie
Dejean	Desjean
Delege	Poirer
Delaurier	Alarie, Delorier, Desloriez, Renaud
Des Carraux	Doram
Desjean	Dejean
Dion	Guitard
Doram	Des Carraux
Drouet	Richardville
Fontenaque	Querry
Gautier	St Germain
Genichon	Canichen, Toulon
German	Lapierre
Guitard	Dion
Jerome	Rejembald
La Coste	Langdo
Laderout	Sequin
Lalamiere	Latumiere, Petit
Lamoureux	St Germain
Lapierre	German
La Tremuille	Millet
La Tulippe	Thierie
Latumiere	Lalumiere, Petite
Langdo	La Coste
Laviolette	Tougas, Violon, Roussian
Levron	Metayer
Levry	Martin
Martin	Levry
Metayer	Levron
Millet	La Tremuille
Petite	Lalumiere, Latumiere
Poirier	Delege
Poitevin	Arpin, Harpin
Preville	Codenoir
Querry	Cary, Fontenaque
Racine	St Marie
Rejembald	Jerome
Renaud	Renau, Renault, Delorier, Desloriez
Roussian	Roufiance, La Violette
St Antoine	Vachet

St Germain	Gautier, Lamoureux
St Jean	Tirard
St Marie	Racine
St Martin	Berton
Schabert	Chapart
Sequin	Laderoute
Thierie	La Tulippe
Tierie	De Fontenac, Querrie
Tirard	St Jean
Tougas	Laviolette
Toulon	Canichen, Genichon
Trempe	Cornouiller, Cornoyer
Vachet	St Antoine
Violon	Laviolette

ST FRANCIS XAVIER CHURCH RECORDS

PARENTAL INFORMATION FROM MARRIAGE RECORDS

1749 - 1838

BY

BARBARA SCHULL WOLFE

Logansport, Ind.

Aug. 1989

Typed By: Rosalie Looker Rowe

NAME   DATE OF MARRIAGE
        PARENTS

Alard, Louis   9-20-1784
        s/o Eustache Alard & Louise Louvin
Amelin, Joseph   1-25-1773
        s/o Laurent Amlin & Magdeleine Gariepi
Amelin, Laurent   5-21-1798
        s/o Laurent Amelin & Matianne La Fleche
Andray, Agate   2-2-1800
        d/o Joseph Andray & Josette Dumay
Andray, Pierre   7-16-1798
        s/o Joseph Andray & Josette Dumay
Andre, Amable   5-2-1831
        s/o Pierre Andre & Josephine Bolon
Andre, Joseph   8-18-1823
        s/o Pierre Andre & Josephine Bolon
Andre, Louise   2-3-1794
        d/o Joseph Andre & Marie Joseph Demais
Andre, Pierre   11-16-1835
        s/o Pierre Andre & Josette Bolon
Andre, Therese   1-7-1796
        d/o Joseph Andre & Josette Dumay
Antara, Marie Josephe   10-17-1763
        d/o Joseph Antara & Marie Joseph Richard
Arpin
        See: Poitevin
Aveline, Laurent   5-28-1808
        s/o Jacques Aveline & Magdeleine Asseline

Babini, Michelange   7-1-1788
        s/o Pierre Babini & Jeanne Leoni
Baillargeon, Nicolas   5-23-1808
        s/o Nicholas Baillargeon & Francoise St Louis
Baillargeon, Victoire   4-25-1820
        d/o Nicolas Baillargeon & Francoise St Louis
Baliarjon, Archeange   10-1-1810
        d/o Nicolas Baliarjon & Francoise St Louis
Baliarjon, Barbe   10-1-1810
        d/o Nicolas Baliarjon & Francoise St Louis
Barada, Antoine   10-23-1759
        s/o Jean Barada & Jeanne Dupin
Barbau, Francois   5-15-1808
        s/o Joseph Barbau & Josephe Paradis
Barbau, Francoise   5-31-1831
        d/o Francois Barbau & Archange Deganne
Baril, Francois   8-30-1786
        s/o Pierre Barril & Marie Anne Bourbeau
Barrois, Francois   2-2-1801
        s/o Francois Barrois & Jannete Ste Marie
Barrois, Lambert   2-23-1789
        s/oFrancois Barrois & Catherine Cecivre

Barrois, Lambert   4-6-1795
        s/o Francois Barrois & Jeanne Cecile
Barrois, Tousaint   1-6-1834
        s/o Joseph Barrois & Therese Godere
Barron, Joseph   2-11-1798 & 5-21-1808
        s/o Pierre Barron & Marie Ann Rayome (Reaume)
Barron, Joseph   8-13-1835
        s/o Joseph Barron & Josephine Gamelin
Barsalou, Jean Bte   8-20-1798
        s/o Nicolas Barsalou & Magdelaine Le Page
Bayard, John Francois   7-7-1823
        s/o Jean Francois Bayard & Susanne Betaux
Bayargeon, Francoise   4-24-1832
        d/o Nicolas Bayargeon & Pelagie Valet
Bayargeon, Pelagie   11-29-1828
        d/o Valletpard Bayargeon & _____
Bayarjon, Francoise   5-23-1796
        d/o Nicolas Bayarjon & Francoise Pluchon
Beaulon, Amable   1-26-1773
        s/o Gabriel Beaulon & Suzanne Menard
Beaulon, Hypolite   9-28-1786
        s/o Gabriel Beaulon & Suzanne Menard
Beauregard, Antoine   1-27-1818
        s/o Jean Bte Beauregard & Lisette Languiran
Belen, Marie Josephe   6-24-1753
        d/o Joseph Belen & Marie Magdeleine St Amend
Benae dit Chartier, Marie Louise 11-8-1813
        d/o Joseph Benae dit Chartier & Marie Louise Girardeau
Bequet, Cecile   1-24-1791
        d/o Pierre Bequet & Catherine Poitiers
Bequet, Francoise   7-25-1796
        d/oPierre Bequet & Catherine Pognet
Bergan, Catherine   4-16-1787
        d/o Dominque Bergan & Marie Josephe Poirer
Bergant, Charles   8-2-1784
        s/o Dominique Bergant & Josephe Deloge
Berthiaume, Angelique   8-2-1784
        d/o Noel Berthiaume & Angelique Toulouse
Berthiome, Noel   8-19-1799
        s/o Noel Berthiome & Angelique Toulouze
Berton dit St Martin, Jean Bte   4-28-1788
        s/o Jean Bte Berton dit St Martin & Therese Mont-habert
Besaillon, Benoit   4-21-1806
        s/o Etienne Besaillon & Anne Robidoux
Bollon, Susanne   5-5-1760
        d/o Gabriel Bollon & Susanne Menard
Boneau, Francoise   8-2-1784
        d/o Charles Boneau & Geneieve Dudevoir
Bonhomme, Charles   11-30-1835
        s/o Jean Bte Bonhomme & Geneieve Villeneuve
Bonhomme, Genevieve   11-23-1818
        d/o Jean Bte Bonhomme & Genevieve Villeneuve

Bonhomme, Jean Bte   4-15-1793
    s/o Michel Bonhomme & Marie Anne Caulombre
Bonhomme, Jeanne   1-6-1834
    d/o Jean Bte Bonhomme & Genevieve Villeneuve
Bonhomme, Michel   10-9-1835
    s/o Jean Bte Bonhomme & Genevieve Villeneuve
Bonneau, Angelique   2-4-1788
    d/o Charles Bonneau & Genevieve Du Devoir
Bonneau, Anne   10-6-1788
    d/o Charles Bonneau & Genevieve Du Devoir
Bonneau, Genevieve   1-14-1773
    d/o Charles Bonneau & Marie Marguerite Dudevoir
Bonneau, Genevieve   3-4-1799
    d/o Charles Bonneau & Genevieve Du Devoir
Bonneau, Jean Baptiste   11-6-1786
    s/o Charles Bonneau & Genevieve Du Devoir
Boneau, Jean Baptiste   10-1-1810
    s/o Jean Baptiste Boneau & Marie Roy (Pacinne indian)
Bonneau, Marie   1-30-1804
    d/o Jean Baptiste Bonneau & Marie Pacane (Miami indian)
Bonneau, Marie Anne   7-7-1823
    d/o Pierre Bonneau & Marie Anne Desnoyans
Bonneau, Pierre   9-19-1785
    s/o Charles Bonneau & Genevieve Du Devoir
Bono, Angelique   4-6-1795
    d/o Charles Bono & Genevieve Du Devoir
Bono, Auguste   4-6-1795
    s/o Charles Bono & Genevieve Du Devoir
Bono, Jeanne   1-21-1833
    d/o Jean Bte Bono & Therese Derosier
Bordelau, Antoine   1-29-1758
    s/o Antoine Bordeleau & Magdeleine Savarie
Bordeleau, Archange   10-3-1785
    d/o Antoine Bordeleau & Catherine Caron
Bordeleau, Catherine   5-23-1808
    d/o Pierre Bordeleau & "Savage Woman"
Bordeleau, Marie Magdeleine   7-9-1779
    d/o Antoine Bordeleau & Catherine Caron
Bordeleau, Michel   7-3-1786
    s/o Antoine Bordeleau & Catherine Carron
Bordeleau, Ursule   5-10-1808
    d/o Michel Bordeleau & Ursule Decouinte
Bosseron, Rose   5-22-1797
    d/o Francois Ridai Bosseron & Francoise Drouet
Bouche, Celeste   5-21-1832
    d/o Joseph Bouche & Archange Tremble
Bouche, Vital   4-24-1832
    s/o Joseph Bouche & Archange Tremble
Boucher, Baptiste   2-3-1818
    s/o Vital Boucher & Marie Cardinal
Boucher, Felix   8-13-1838
    s/o Jean Boucher & Marie Raiscot

Boucher, Francois   9-19-1820
    s/o Vital Boucher & Josette Cardinal
Boucher, Jean Baptiste   9-17-1811
    s/o Vital Boucher & Josette Cardinal
Boucher, Joseph   6-13-1814
    s/o Joseph Boucher & Marguerite Lafource
Boucher, Julie   6-13-1814
    d/o Vital Boucher & Marie Cardinal
Boucher, Suzanne   2-3-1818
    d/o Vital Boucher & Marie Cardinal
Boucher, Vital   5-2-1785
    s/o Jean Bte Boucher & Catherine Glatis
Boulon, Josette   7-16-1798
    d/o Amable Boulon & Josette Godere
Bourdeloux, Ignace   2-14-1825
    s/o Michel Bourdeloux & Ursule Decointe
Bourdeloux, Michel   10-26-1825
    s/o Michel Bourdeloux & Ursule Decointe
Boye, Francois   4-24-1792
    s/o Louis Boye & Marie Ann Gauder
Boyer, Francois   5-17-1808
    s/o Louis Boyer & Marie Anne Goder
Boyer, Jean Baptiste   2-3-1794
    s/o Louis Boyer & Marianne Gaudere
Boyer, Louis   1-8-1789
    s/o Louis Boyer & Marie Anne Codere
Boyer, Ursule   8-4-1794
    d/o Louis & Marianne Gaudere
Brossard, Joseph   2-25-1789
    s/o Urbain Brossard & Francoise Coquillard
Brouillet, Barbe   7-4-1796
    d/o Michel Brouillet & Barbe Boneau
Brouillette Marianne   8-13-1835
    d/o Michel Brouillette & Marie Louise Derouette
Brouillet, Michel   9-21-1811
    s/o Michel Brouillet & Barbe Bonneau
Brouillet, Pierre   6-13-1814
    s/o Michel Brouillet & Barbe Bonneau
Brouillete, Pierre   2-18-1833
    s/o Michel Brouillete & Marie Louise Richarville

Cabassier, Adelaide   7-6-1818
    d/o Charlot Cabassier & Marie Louise Mallet
Cabassier, Charles   1-30-1792
    s/o Louis Cabassier & Victoire G. Daune
Cabassier, Pierre   11-20-1797
    s/o Charles Cabassier & Marie Louise Mallet
Cadoret, Francois   1-28-1802
    s/o Francois Cadoret & Ursule Bigras
Caloutre, Jean Bte   3-4-1799
    s/o Louis Caloutre & Josette Godin

Campeau, Francois   5-8-1786
    s/o Michel Campeau & Marie Josephe Buteau
Campau, Francoise   2-14-1825
    d/o Remy Campau & Helene Grimard
Campeau, Genevieve   12-11-1809
    d/o Rene Campeau & Helene Grimard
Campeau, Helene   10-1-1810
    d/o Rene Campeau & Helene Grimard
Campeau, Jeanne   10-1-1810
    d/o Rene Campeau & Helene Grimard
Canichon
    See: Toulon
Cardinal, Barbe   7-15-1805
    d/o Jacques Cardinal & Barbe Deligne -(Edeline)
Cardinal, Celeste   6-13-1796
    d/o Jean Baptiste Cardinal & Marie Anne Malette
Cardinal, Felicite   10-1-1810
    d/o Nicholas Cardinal & Marie Josette Girard
Cardinal, Francois   5-23-1808
    s/o Nicolas Cardinal & Marie Josephine Girard
Cardinal, Henrietta   10-1-1810
    d/o Jacques Cardinal & Barbe Edeline
Cardinal, Jacques   8-2-1784
    s/o Jean Bte Cardinal & Marieanne Mallet
Cardinal, Jean Baptiste   12-11-1809
    s/o Jacques Cardinal & Barbe Edeline
Cardinal, Jeanne   4-10-1795
    d/o Jean Bte Cardinal & Marianne Mallet
Cardinal, Joseph   11-26-1806
    s/o Nicolas Cardinal & Josephine Girard
Cardinal, Marie   11-23-1806
    d/o Jacques Cardinal & Barbe Deligne
Cardinal, Marie Felicite   1-2-1792
    d/o Nicolas Cardinal & Marie Josette Girard
Cardinal, Marie Francoise   2-19-1787
    d/o Nicolas Cardinal & Marie Josephe Girard
Cardinal, Marie Jeanne   1-16-1773
    d/o Jean Bte Cardinal & Marie Anne Mallet
Cardinal, Marie Josephe   5-2-1785
    d/o Nicolas Cardinal & Marie Josephe Girard
Cardinal, Nicolas   1-7-1761
    s/o Jacques Cardinal & Marie Jeanne Dugue
Cardinal, Nicolas   5-10-1808
    s/o Nicolas Cardinal & Marie Josephine Girard
Cardinal, Theresa   5-2-1785
    d/o Nicholas Cardinal & Marie Josephe Girard
Cardinal, Toussaint   1-12-1835
    s/o Nicolas Cardinal & Ursule Dauning (Danis)
Caron, Catherine   1-29-1758
    d/o Vital Caron & Magdeleine Pruneau
Caron, Louise   1-25-1757
    d/o Vital Caron & Magdeleine Pruneau
Carretier, Susanne   10-19-1818
    d/o Pierre Carretier & Veronique Mallet

Cartier, Isadore   4-25-1820
        s/o Pierre Cartier & Veronique Mallet
Cartier, Marie Magdelene   9-17-1811
        d/o Pierre Cartier & Veronique Mallet
Casse See: St Aubin
Cayon, Francois   7-24-1797
        s/o Pierre Cayon & Veronique Guitard
Chabot, Bernard   5-15-1808
        s/o Joseph Charbot & Ursule Clemont
Chabot, Cecile   5-21-1793
        d/o Joseph Chabot & Ursule Clemont
Chabot, Francoise   11-27-1834
        d/o Bernard Chabot & Therese Renaud
Chabot, Joseph   1-18-1773
        s/o Pierre Chabot & Cecile Jouaine
Chamberlaine dit Germain, Therese 9-24-1810
        d/o Louis Chamberlain & Marie Beauvais
Chapa, Auguste   10-12-1818
        s/o Nicolas Chapa & Cecile Langdoc
Chapard, Antoine   11-19-1806
        s/o Nicolas Chapard & Cecile La Coste
Chapart, Marie Claire   6-20-1785
        d/o Nicholas Chapart & Marie Claire Staeler
Chapart, Nicholas   7-19-1784
        s/o Nicholas Chapard & Marie Claire Allemond
Chappart
    See : Lefevre and Schabart
Chartier
    See : Benae
Chartier, Genevieve   6-2-1794
        d/o Joseph Chartier & Marie Louise Girardeau
Choteau, Marie Julie   4-21-1806
        d/o Auguste Choteau & Francoise Volsay
Clermont, Ursule (widow of Francois Le Cointe) 1-18-1773
        d/o Louis Clermont & Louise Bauron
Codenoir
    See: Preville
Codere
    See: Gauder - Godere
Codere, Agnes   8-2-1784
        d/o Louis Codere & Barbe Lerond
Codere, Genevieve   2-13-1786
        d/o Pierre Codere & Susanne Beaulon
Codere, Marguerite   8-2-1784
        d/o Francois Codere & Marguerite Chapard
Codere, Rene   2-13-1786
        s/o Rene Codere & Catherine Campeau
Compagnot, Elizabeth   11-16-1835
        d/o Pierre Compagnot & Marguerite Gamelin
Compagnot, Francoise   1-23-1800
        d/o Francois Compagnot & Marianne Cardinal
Compagnot, Marie Anne   11-15-1787
        d/o Francois Compagnot & Marie Anne Romagou

Compagnot, Marie Therese   1-18-1773
        d/o Francois Compagnot & Marieanne Romugen
Compagnot, Pierre   5-28-1808
        s/o Francois Compagnot & Marieanne Cardinal
Compo, Catherine   3-31-1761
        d/o Nicolas Compo & Agate St Aubin
Compo, Victoire   2-18-1833
        d/o Michel Compo & Marie Baillarjon
Cornoullier, Angelique   9-6-1811
        d/o Pierre Cornoullier & Angelique Racine
Cornoullier, Antoine   9-24-1810
        s/o Pierre Cornoullier & Angelique Racine
Cornoyer, Helene   1-12-1835
        d/o Antoine Cornoyer & Therese Chamberlan dit Germain
Coulter, Matilda   12-26-1819
        d/o Thomas Coulter & Mary Doleur
Cournoier, Angelique   10-26-1825
        d/o Ambroise Cournoier & Therese Derorier
Cournoiullier, Genevieve   10-1-1810
        d/o Pierre Cournoiullier & Angelique Racine
Cournoyier, Ambroise   12-1-1806
        s/o Pierre Cournoyier & Angelique Racine
Cournoyer, Genevieve   2-13-1786
        d/o Pierre Cournoyer & Angelique Racine
Cournoyer, Helene   9-19-1785
        d/o Pierre Cournoyer & Angelique Racine
Crely, Charlot   7-6-1818
        s/o Jerome Crely & Therese Lefevre
Creley, Francoise   11-26-1806
        d/o Jerome Crely & Therese Lefevre
Crely, Jerome   8-2-1785
        s/o Jean Bte Crely & Angelique Pilet
Crepeau, Catherine   1-18-1773
        d/o Louis Crepeau & Mary Louise Perthius
Custeaud, Jean Bte   11-28-1802
        s/o Jean Bte Custeaud & Genevieve St Jean

Dagenay, Ambroise   1-21-1773
        s/o Joseph Dagenay & Marie Josephe Charest
Dagnay, Victoire   6-13-1803
        d/o Joseph Dagnay & Monique Moran
Dagenet, Mary   9-27-1819
        d/o Ambroise Dagenet & Mary (of Miamis)
Daher, Elizabeth   5-23-1808
        d/o Jean Bte Daher & Sale
Daigniaux, Louis Toussaint   1-24-1791
        s/o Louis Dayniaux & Angelique Ganie
Daniel, Elizabeth   5-2-1831
        d/o Pierre Daniel & Elizabeth (Bery)
Danis, Marie Louise   2-23-1789
        d/o Honore Danis & Marie Louise (Butos)
Danis, Ursule   5-10-1808
        d/o Laurent Danis & Joesphine Goder

Danys, Marguerite   8-2-1784
        d/o Honre Dany & Louise (Butos)
Daplond, Guillaume   4-4-1796
        s/o Guillaume Daplond & Marie Louise (Daperon) Clermont
Dauphin, Jean Bte   9-11-1820
        s/o Barthelemy Dauphin & Charlotte Duret
De Fontenac
    See: Tierie
De Gane, Archange   8-16-1802 & 5-15-1808
        d/o Joseph De Gane & Madeleine Prudhomme
De Gane, Joseph   8-5-1799
        s/o Joseph De Gane & Catherine Menard
Dejarlais, Eloi   5-23-1808
        s/o Joseph Dejarlais & Josephine Harvien
Dejean   See: Desjean
Dejean, Clorisse   11-23-1818
        d/o Philippe Dejean & Victoire Cournoyer
Dejean, Phillipe   7-21-1794
        s/o Phillipe Dejean & Angelique Angers
Delaurer
    See: Renau and Delorier
Deligne, Francoise   1-30-1832
        d/o Joseph Deligne & Genevieve Delorier
Deligne, Marie Louise   2-15-1791
        d/o Louis Deligne & Marie Thomas
Delille, Cecille   2-22-1819
        d/o Charles Delille & Jeanette Barcelot
Delile, Charlotte   7-14-1793
        d/o Amable Delile & Marie Josephe (Meloche)
Delille, Josette   6-19-1820
        d/o Charles Delille & Agate Litalien
Delile, Marie Josephine   4-6-1795
        d/o Amable Delile & Marie Josephine Meloche
Delisle, Cecile   5-28-1808
        d/o Charles Delisle & Jeanne Barcelleau (Barxlolux)
Delisle, Charles   2-2-1800
        s/o Charles Deliale & Marie Chuvin
Delisle, Charles   5-30-1814
        s/o Charles Delisle & Jeanne Bordeleau
Delisle, Jean Bte   10-19-1818
        s/o Chrlot Delisle & Jeannette Bercelot
Delisle, Victoire   12-25-1809
        d/o Charles Delisle & Jeanne Bercelon
Delories
    See: Renard
Deloriers, Francois Xavier   8-7-1820
        s/o Jean Bte Deloriers & Marie Magdeleine (Bordeleau)
Delorier, Louis   8-2-1784
        s/o Jean Bte Renaud Delorier & Therese Mallet
Delorier, Marie   10-9-1835
        d/o Pierre Delorier & Marie Ravalette
De Mers, Pierre   2-25-1775
        s/o Pierre De Mers & Marie Josephe Rousianthis

Denaud
   See: Deneau & Deslaurier
Deanlau, Angelique   5-30-1814
       d/o Toussaint Deneau & Cecile Bequet
Deneau, Francoise   5-30-1808
       d/o Louis Deneau dit Deslaurier
Deneau, Toussaint   11-19-1806 & 11-8-1813
       s/o Charles Deneau & Barbe Moison or Moyson
Denie, Marie Louise   10-19-1760
       d/o Jacques Denie & Maeie Louise Deligne
Denis
   See: Danys
Denot, Barbe   10-12-1818
       d/o Rene Denot & Cecile Sequin
Denoyon, Angelique   11-19-1806
       d/o Louis Denoyon & Marie Anne La Fleur
Denoyon, Barbe   11-19-1806
       d/o Louis Denoyon & Marie Anne La Fleur
Denoyon, Francoise   7-9-1798
       d/o Louis DeNoyon & Marianne Palu
Denoyon, Jean Louis   1-19-1761
       s/o Jean Bte Denoyon & Louise Blin
Dequinte, Marie   9-19-1820
       d/o Jean Bte Dequinte & Marie Bready
Desbiens, Andre   1-24-1803
       s/o Joseph Desbiens & Therese Teaier
Desbiens, Helene   7-19-1828
       d/o Richard Desbiens & _____
Des Carraux
   See: Doram
Desjardins, Hiacynthe   1-24-1803
       s/o Louis Desjardins & Louise Gauthier
Desjean
   See: Dejean
Desjean, Julie   11-1-1819
       d/o Philippe Desjean & Victoire Cournoyer
Deslaurier - Deslorier
   See: Delorier - Deneau - Renaud
Desloriez, Desanges   7-6-1801
       d/o Jean Bte Renaud dit Desloriez & Madelwinw Bordeleau
Desloriez, Eleanore   7-6-1801
       d/o Renaud dit Deslorier & Marguerite Godere
Desloriers, Jean Bte Renault   7-9-1799
       s/o Jean Bte Renault Deslauriers & Therese Mallet
Deslorier, Marieanne   8-14-1818
       d/o Jean Bte Deslorier & Marie Madeleine Bordeleau
Desnaux, Rene   2-10-1800
       s/o Charles Desnaux & Barbe Mayson
Des Noyons, Magquerite   4-27-1807
       d/o Louis De Noyons & Marie Anne Palu
Des Riviers, Julian Trottier   4-21-1749
       s/o Julian Trottier Des Riviers & _____

Desrouchers, Joseph   2-27-1770
     s/o Jean Desrouchers & Marie Veaudrie
Desrosiers, Marguerite   10-23-1759
     d/o Bonnavanture Desrosiers & Marguerite Durivage
Desrosier, Pelagie   10-1-1810
     d/o Bonaventure Desrosier & Marie Louise Lefevre
Desvegnets, Marie   7-18-1779
     d/o Nicolas Desvegnets & Dorothy Mercier
Detailly, Joseph   10-16-1786
     s/o Joseph Detailly & Marie Anne Lafontaine
Devegnais, Marie Anne   8-3-1789
     d/o Jacques Devegnais & Marie Anne Sequin
De Villers, Marie Josephe   2-29-1787
     d/o Jean Bte De Villers & Marie Victoire Huneau
Disi, Michel   4-23-1763
     s/o Pierre Disi & Therese Roux
Dolehun, John   1-30-1820
     s/o Daniel Dolehun & Helena Dowd
Doram dit Des Carraux, Francoise   2-14-1820
     d/o Andre Doram dit Des Carraux & Theresa Beaulieu
Drouet
   See: Richardville
Duboise, Etienne   11-23-1806
     s/o Jean Bte Duboise & Rose Larzelle (Labelle)
Duboise, Joseph   8-4-1794
     s/o Charles Duboise & Geneieve Victor
Duboise, Toussaint   10-6-1788
     s/o Charles Duboise & Cecile Courret
Dudevoir, Anne   11-23-1756
     d/o Claude Dudevoir & Barbe Cardinal
Du Devoir, Geneieve   12-1-1806
     d/o Charles Du Devoir & Agnes Boyer
Dunais
   See: De Mers
Dupre, Louis   2-16-1801
     s/o Louis Dupre & Elizabeth La Liberte

Edeline, Francois Xavier Joseph   2-12-1799
     s/o Louis Edeline & Marie Thomas
Edeline, Joseph   2-22-1819
     s/o Louis Edeline & Marie Thomas
Edeline, Marie Josephe   7-24-1778
     d/o Louis Edeline & Marie Thomas
Edeline, Nicolas   8-10-1795
     s/o Louis Edeline & Marie Thomas
Edelyne, Barbe   8-2-1784
     d/o Louis Edelyne & Marie Thomas
Ester, Joseph
     s/o Pierre Ester & Marie Magdeleine Heler

Fiot, Joseph   5-23-1808
    s/o Claude Fiot & Catherine Pilet

Galvin, Elizabeth   5-23-1808
    d/o Nicolas Galvin & Elonore Gottin
Gamelin, Elizabeth   1-16-1820
    d/o Paul Gamelin & Marguerite Derouet
Gamelin, Josephine   5-21-1808
    d/o Pierre Gamelin & Ursule Vaudri
Gamelin, Marguerite   5-28-1808
    d/o Paul Gamelin & Marguerite Derouet (Richardville)
Gamelin, Paul   6-6-1785
    s/o Lawrence Gamelin & Josephe Du Devoir
Gamelin, Pierre   7-24-1778
    s/o Laurent Gamelin & Josephe Dudevoir
Gamelin, Pierre   11-15-1813
    s/o Pierre Gamelin & Ursule Vaudri
Ganichon - Ganichou
    See: Toulon
Garcia, Jean (spaniard)   11-19-1788
    s/o Jean Garcia & Baltazard Doming
Gauder
    See: Codere - Godere
Gauder, Marie Josephe   1-26-1773
    d/o Francoise Godere & Agnes Richard
Gaudere, Felicite   5-23-1793
    d/o Louis Gaudere & Barbe Metayer
Gauder, Rene   3-3-1761
    s/o Francois Gauder & Agnes Richard
Gaudere, Pierre   5-5-1760
    s/o Francois Gaudere & Agnes Richard
Gaudere, Vivtoire   7-14-1794
    d/o Rene Gaudere & Catherine Campeau
Gendron, Jean Bte   7-25-1796
    s/o Joseph Gendron & Josette de Gray
Genereux, Francois   5-21-1832
    s/o Joseph Genereux & Francoise _____
Genier, Honore   5-18-1814
    d/o Honore Genier & Therese Pepin
Germain
    See: Chamberlain & Lapierre
Girard, Marie Josephe   1-7-1761
    d/o Jean Bte Girard & Marie Josephe Raimond
Girardin, Auguste   5-23-1808
    s/o Michel Girardin & Marie St Jean
Girardin, Jean Bte   5-31-1831
    s/o Augustin Girardin & Catherine Bordeleau
Giroud, Laurent   7-4-1795
    s/o Pierre Giroud & Marie Snegal
Godere
    See: Codere & Gauder

Goder, Francois   1-18-1773
        s/o Francois Gauder & Agnes Richard
Godere, Francois   1-30-1804
        s/o Louis Godere & Barbe Levrond
Godere, Henri Pierre   7-9-1798
        s/o Pierre Godere & Suzanne Boulon
Godaire, Pierre   1-30-1832 & 10-2-1837
        s/o Pierre Godaire & Marie Asex - Assix
Godere, Marie Louise   1-28-1802
        d/o Louis Godere & Barbe Levron
Godere, Therese   8-10-1795
        d/o Francois Godere & Theresa Compagnot
Godere, Victoire   2-2-1801 & 7-15-1805
        d/o Francois Godere & Marie Theresa Compagnot
Gonzales, Simon (spanard)   2-27-1798
        s/o Jacques Gonzales & Angela Merino du Royaume
Goyaut, Paul   11-27-1834
        s/o Louison Goyaut & Barbe Mallet
(Great Louis), Cecile   2-11-1798
        d/o Great Louis (indian) & Marguerite ___ (indian)
        (She married Joseph Barron)
Grimard, Charles   12-19-1808
        s/o Pierre Girmard & Geneieve Compagnot
Grimard, Charles   1-29-1835
        s/o Pierre Grimard & Josephine Deligne
Grimard, Geneieve   7-6-1795
        d/o Pierre Grimard & Geneieve Collon
Grimard, Geneieve   1-7-1819
        d/o Pierre Grimard & Josette Delile
Grimard, Heleine   5-8-1786
        d/o Pierre Grimard & Geneieve Compagnotte
Grimard, Pierre   4-6-1795
        s/o Pierre Grimard & Geneieve Coulon
Guele, Charles   4-4-1796
        s/o Charles Guele & Elizabeth Clermont
Guelle, Josephine   7-14-1805
        d/o Charles Guelle & Elizabeth Clermont
Guelle, Marie   11-8-1813
        d/o Charles Guelle & Elizabeth Clermont
Guinel, Francois   6-29-1794
        s/o Francois Guinel & Catherine Barito

Harpin
   See: Poitevin
Harvin, Jean   7-19-1793
        s/o Leonard Harvin & Marie Louise _____
Hunot, Joseph   11-23-1818
        s/o Gabriel Hunot & Marguerite Cournoyer
Hunot, Magdeleine   8-20-1787
        d/o Joseph Hunot & De Marie Josephe Robert
Hunot, Pelagie   7-19-1819
        d/o Gabriel Hunot & Marie Ann Compagnot

Jacob, Marguerite   5-23-1808
    d/o Christian Jacob & _____
Jacqueau, Marie Helene   4-4-1796
    d/o Etinne Jacqueau & Marie Louise Carra
Jenkins, George Mary   9-12-1836
    s/o Thomas Jenkins & Charlotte _____ (colored)
Joyeuse, Francoise   6-2-1832
    s/o Joseph Joyeuse & Celeste Cardinal
Joyeux, Guillaume   2-14-1820
    s/o Joseph Joyeux & Celeste Cardinal
Joyeuse, Joseph   2-15-1791
    s/o Francois Joyeuse & Marie Larouse
Joyeux, Joseph   6-13-1796
    s/o Francois Joyeux & Marie Demoulin

Kyout, Louis   5-9-1831
    s/o Louis Kyout & Marie Constance

La Belle, Catherine   10-16-1786
    d/o Claude La Belle & _____
La Buxiera, Charles Joseph   2-13-1786
    s/o Charles Joseph La Buxiera & Marie Ann Vifarraine
Lacoste, Andre   1-25-1773
    s/o Andre Lacoste & Marie Boutin
Lacoste, Angelique   1-28-1773
    d/o Francois Lacoste & Magdeleine Bouron
La Coste, Cecilia   7-19-1784
    d/o Francois La Coste & Marie Bouron
Lacoste, Joseph   1-30-1832
    s/o Charles Lacoste & Ursule Bordeleau
Lacoste dit Langdo, Julie   5-6-1833
    d/o Andre Lacoste & Babee Baillarjon
Lacroix, Dominique   9-3-1821
    s/o Dominique Lacroix & Geneieve Berthelette
La Deroute
    See: Sequin
La Feuillade
    See: Le Feuillade
La Feuillade, Charlotte   7-24-1786
    d/o Joseph La Feuillade & Marie Anne Emelin -(Amelin)
La Feuillade, Marianne   7-17-1797 & 8-5-1799
    d/o Joseph La Feuillade & Marianne Emelin - (Amelin)
La Feuillade, Pierre   7-14-1794
    s/o Joseph La Feuillade & Marianne Amelin (Emelin)
Laffont, Marie   4-18-1786
    d/o Jean Baptiste Laffont & Charlotte La Course
La Fontaine, Catherine   6-20-1795
    d/o Etienne La Fontaine & Catherine St Aubix - Aubin
La Fontain, Marguerite   6-29-1794
    d/o Etienne La Fontaine & Catherine St Aubin
Laforet, Marianne   9-11-1820
    d/o Pierre Laforet & Archange Deganns

Laforest, Pierre   2-6-1770
    s/o Pierre Laforest & Josephe Buret
Laforet, Pierre   8-16-1802
    s/o Pierre Laforet & Marie Anne Emelin
Lagarde, Marie   9-9-1811
    d/o Jean Baptiste Lagarde & Angelique Ravalet
La Lumier
  See: Petit
Lamote, Joseph   11-24-1793
    s/o Joseph Lamote & Marie Hubert
Langdo
  See: Lacoste
Lamoureaux, Magdeleine St Germain   3-19-1770
    d/o Pierre St Germain Lamoureaux & Felicite Chavegnon
Langlois, Jannete   10-26-1795
    d/o Francois Langlois & Magdelaine Prudent
Langlois, Jean Bte   7-15-1805
    s/o Francois Langlois & Magdeleine Prudhomme
Languedoc, Andre   10-1-1810
    s/o Francois Languedoc & Therese Compagnot
Languedoc, Charles   5-10-1808
    s/o Francois Languedoc & Therese Godere
Lapierre dit Germain, Marguerite   10-3-1788
    d/o Jean Lapierre & Marie Marthe
Laplante, Pierre   1-16-1820
    s/o Jean Bte Laplante & Marie Carnson
Larche, Marguerite   11-28-1802
    d/o Joseph Larche & Annable Sara
La Rue, Catherine   11-19-1788
    d/o _____ La Rue & Elizabeth Bineau
Latour, Augustin   1-25-1819
    s/o Joseph Latour & Angelique Leveille
Latour, Henry   6-19-1820
    s/o Pierre Latour & Geneieve Cornoyer
Latour, Pierre   2-13-1786
    s/o Pierre Latour & Catherine Denis
Latrimouille
  See: Millet
Latremouille, Marie   5-23-1808
    d/o Jacques Latremouille & Marie Lefevne (La Fleur)
La Tulippe
  See: Querie & Thiere
La Violette
  See: Roussian
Laviolette, Marguerite   1-25-1819
    d/o Louison Laviolette dit Violon & Jeannette Crystome
Laviolette, Marie Therese Roufiance dit   1-26-1773
    d/o Francois Roufiance dit Laviolette & Marie Anne Poineau
Le Cointe, Ursule   7-3-1786
    d/o Francois Le Cointe & Ursule Clermont
Lefebvre, Antoine   1-25-1757
    s/o Laurent Lefebvre & Marie Geneieve Bodin

Lefeuillade, Angelique   8-2-1784
    d/o Joseph Lefeuillade & Maeianne Ameline
LeFeuillade
  See: La Feuillade
Lefevre, Antoine   1-21-1788
    s/o Antoine Lefevre & Marie Louise Caron
Lefevre, Marie Ann Chappart dit   1-29-1835
    d/o Antoine Lefevre & Marie Query
Lefevre, Theresa   8-2-1785
    d/o Antoine Lefevre & Louise Caron
Legarde, Marie Louise   5-21-1798
    d/o Jean Bte Legarde & Marianne Ravalette
Le Grand, Delle Veronique   7-1-1788
    d/o Gabriel Le Grand & Veronique Reaume
Le Gras, John Marie   7-18-1779
    s/o Jean Bte Le Gras & Geneieve Gamelin
Le Pointe, Catherine   1-8-1789
    d/o Joseph Le Pointe & Marie Louise _____
Leveyer, Rosalie   9-12-1836
    d/o Louis Leveyer & Rosanne _____ (colored)
Levron, Veronique   11-30-1835
    d/o Antoine Levron & Antoinette Asher
Levron, Victoire   12-9-1809
    d/o Joseph Levron & Celeste Cardinal
Levry dit Martin, Pierre   2-19-1787
    s/o Martin Levry & Angelique Descamps Labadie
Lionois, Jean Baptiste   8-2-1784
    s/o Jean Bte Lionois & Angelique Dudevoir
Lognion - Lognon
  See: Loyon
Lognon, Louis   10-1-1810
    s/o Francois Louis Lognon & Marie Josette Girard
Lognon (Logan), Marie   1-23-1832
    d/o Louis Loyon & Henriette Cardinal
Loyon, Charles   7-14-1793
    s/o Francois Loyon & Marianne Dube

Mc Cay, Robert   4-18-1786
    s/o Robert Mc Cay & Anne Waters

Maillot
  See: Mayot
Malboeuf, Jean Moise   10-3-1788
    s/o Pierre Malboeuf & Marie Moyen
Mallet, Ambroise   9-6-1811
    s/o Pierre Mallet & Angelique Major Beautron
Mallet, Angelique   1-20-1794
    d/o Pierre Mallet & Angelique Botron
Mallet, Elizabeth   2-27-1786
    d/o Pierre Mallet & Marie Magdalene Beautron

Mallet, Francois   8-14-1818
    s/o Guillaume Mallet & Marie Josette
Malet, Francoise   11-20-1797
    d/o Francois Malet & Marie Charles Metayer (Levron)
Mallet, Geneieve   10-2-1837
    d/o Louis Mallet & Geneieve Querret de Fontenac
Mallet, Louis   5-23-1808
    s/o Pierre Mallet & Angelique Beautron
Mallet, Marie Louise   1-30-1792
    d/o Francois Mallet & Marie Charlotte Levront
Mallet, Rose   7-19-1793
    d/o Francois Mallet & Charlotte Leveron
Mallet, Theresa   5-8-1786
    d/o Francois Mallet & Charlotte Levron dit Metayer
Malette, Therese   10-26-1750
    d/o Antoine Malette & Theresa Mayotte
Mallette, Virginie   4-8-1833
    d/o Francois Mallette & Cecile Alarie
Mangin, Marie Louise   1-28-1760
    d/o Francois Mangin & Marie Angelique Dudevoir
Marchal, Antoine   5-22-1797
    s/o Jacques Marchal & Jeanne Sellier
Marie, Josette   4-21-1794
    d/o Antoine Marie & Marianne Checamihe
Martin
  See: Levry
Mayot (Maillot), Nicolas   8-3-1789
    s/o Nicolas Mayot & Clotilda Brisson
Mellieur, Francois   9-9-1811
    s/o Francois Mellieur & Marguerite Lecuyer
Menon, Pierre   1-28-1760
    s/o Francois Menon & Anne Nourri
Metai, Joseph   11-8-1813
    s/o Joseph Metai & Charlotte La Fayliade
Mete, Joseph   7-24-1786
    s/o Joseph Mete & Catherine Du Four
Mete, Magdeleine   5-7-1821
    d/o Joseph Mete & Charlotte Lafeuillade
Metis, Pierre   10-2-1820
    s/o Joseph Meti & Charlotte Laoillade
Millet dit Latrimouille, Jacques   2-14-1771
    s/o Jacques Millet dit Latrimouille & Marie Lafleur
Millet, Jean Baptiste   2-26-1775
    s/o Francois Millet & Catherine Le Due
Millet dit La Tremouille, Rosalie 8-20-1798
    d/o Jacques Millet dit Tremouille & Marie La Fleur
Miyot, _____   4-6-1795
         d/o _____ Miyot & _____ Gibault
Moise - Moyse, Jean Bte   7-6-1795
    s/o Charles Moise & Catherine St Aubin
Momeni, Antoine   1-13-1834
    s/o Jean Bte Momeni & Marguerite Lavalette
Momenil, Joseph   1-7-1833
    s/o Jean Bte Momenil & Marguerite Ravalette

Mominy, Jean   8-16-1802
    s/o Louis Mominy & Agate Prushomme
Mondou, Martial   5-7-1821
    s/o Jean Mondou & Jeanne Barbe
Montplaiser, Andre   4-10-1795
    s/o Nicolas Montplaiser & Magdeleine La Coste
Moyse, Charles (Moise)   5-23-1796
    s/o Charles Moyse & Catherine St Aubin
Moyse - Moise, Charlot   1-7-1819
    s/o Charlot Moyse & Francoise Bayargeon
Moyse - Moise, Maire Anne   1-17-1835
    d/o Charles Moyse & Francoise Baliarjon(see; baptism)
Munier, Jean   11-4-1793
    s/o Pierre Munier & Anne Barron

Novel, Hypolite   5-28-1808
    s/o Francois Noval & Amable Rayome
Noyes, Jean Baptiste   10-1-1810
    s/o Charles Noyes & Catherine St Aubin
Noyon, Louis   7-27-1795
    s/o Louis Noyon & Marianne Palu

O'neille, Joseph   12-25-1809
    s/o Pierre O'Neille & Jenetie Chandonais
Ouillete, Agate   2-25-1775
    d/o Jean Bte Ouillette & Agate Marion

Page, Dominic   12-19-1809
    s/o Guillaume Page & Marie Huneau
Page, Guillaume   2-26-1770 & 7-26-1778
    s/o Francois Page & Marguerite Laroche
Page, Josette   5-14-1798
    d/o Guillaume Page & Josette Charpart
Page, Madeleine   1-24-1803
    d/o Guillaume Page & Marie Victoire Hunaud
Page Marie   2-27-1798
    d/o Guillaume Page & Marie Huno
Pageix, Marie Josephe   11-24-1793
    d/o Guillaume Pageix & Josephe Chappart
Paille, Joseph   3-19-1770
    s/o Gabriel Paille & Marie Guillemot
Pallu, Marie Amable   1-19-1761
    d/o Pierre Pallu & Angelique Lecomte
Paquin, Francois   7-5-1786
    s/o Pierre Paquin & Cecile St Ange
Peckhem, Lewis   9-27-1819
    s/o Thomas Peckhem & Anna Weaver
Pelletier, Pierre   7-15-1805
    s/o Francois Pelletier & Felicite Miniot
Peltier, Andre   1-28-1773
    s/o Joseph Peltier & Marie Anne Rocher

Perodeau, Angelique			2-26-1775
	d/o Joseph Perodeau & Marie Angelique Pallu
Perodot, Barbe			4-28-1788
	d/o Joseph Perodot & Angelique Palu
Perron, Jeanne			2-27-1770
	d/o Pierre Perron & Francoise Desfouries
Perron, Pierre			1-26-1773
	s/o Pierre Perron & Francoise Fournelle
Perrot, Nicolas			7-24-1778
	s/o Etienne Perrot & Marieanne Guenet
Perthius, Louise			11-26-1749
	d/o Nicolas Perthius & Louise Chauvin
Perthius Pierre			1-3-1757
	s/o Pierre Perthius & Angelique Vital
Petit dit La Lumiere, Antoine	2-29-1787
	s/o Michel Petite dit La Lumiere & Marie Magdeleine
						Petaillier
Petite dit Lalumiere, Antonie	10-19-1818
	s/o Antoine Petite & Josette Villerais
Petite dit Lalumiere, Heleonore	10-23-1820
	d/o Antoine Petite & Josette Villeret
Petite dit Lalumiere, Henriette	9-3-1821
	d/o Antoine Petite & Josette Villere
Picard, Alexis			10-23-1820
	s/o Alexis Picard & Janette Racine
Pinsoneau, Etienne			9-29-1794
	s/o Paschel Pinsoneau & Marguerite Bourdeau
Pitcher, John			12-26-1819
	s/o John Pitcher & Elizabeth Along
Poidevin, Francois			7-6-1818
	s/o Francois Poidevin & Therese Menac - Benac
Potdevin, Susanne			5-9-1831
	d/o Francois Potdevin & Therese Benac
Poirier, Paul			11-4-1794
	s/o Charles Poirier & Marie Demouchet
Poirier dit Deloge, Pierre		10-17-1785
	s/o Pierre Bte Poirier & Geneieve Deschamps
Potevin, Catherine			10-8-1810
	d/o Jean Bte Potevin & Geneieve Lepont
Poitevin dit Arpon, Francois	6-2-1794
	s/o Jean Bte Poitevin dit Arpen (Harpin) & Geneieve Perron
Potevin, Marie			7-24-1797
	d/o Jean Bte Potevin & Geneieve Perron
Pothier, Catherine			9-20-1784
	d/o Charles Pothier & Catherine Poudret
Preville dit Codenoir, Louis	5-8-1786
	s/o Louis Preville dit Codenoir & Magdalene Paventeau

Querie
  See: Thiere - Tierie
Querre, Geneieve			5-23-1808
	d/o Pierre Querre & Angelique Borneau

Querrey, Geneieve   10-27-1818
    d/o Pierre Querrey & Marie Entaya
Quere, Pierre   10-17-1763
    s/o Pierre Quere & Marie Anne Lefevre
Querre, Therese   3-3-1800
    d/o Pierre Querre & Marie Josephe Antagnac

Racicot
  See: Rasicot
Racico, Antoine   6-23-1832
    s/o Francois Racico & Francoise Compagnotte
Racicot, Marie   2-3-1818
    d/o Francois Racicot & Francoise Compagnotte
Racico, Sylvester   9-3-1832
    s/o Francois Racico & Francoise Compagnotte
Racine
  See: St Marie
Racine, Andre   5-21-1793
    s/o Jean Bte Racine & Jeanne Du Devoir
Racine, Cecile   8-7-1820
    d/o Andre Racine & Cecile Charlotte (Chabot)
Racine dit St Marie, Celeste   10-8-1803
    d/o Francois Racine & Marie Therese Compagnot
Racine, Jean Bte   11-23-1756
    s/o Louis Racine & Louise Lavasseur
Racine, Jean Bte   7-3-1820
    s/o Francois Racine & Marie Therese Compagnotte
Racine, Marie Louise   5-22-1785
    d/o Francois (Jean Bte) Racine & Anne Du Devoir
Racine, Marie Therese   9-20-1802
    d/o Francois Racine & Marie Therese Compagnot
Racuse, Marianne   1-30-1832
    d/o Manuel Racuse & Jeanette Campo
Raimbault, Pierre   7-27-1779
    s/o Charles Raimbault & Julia Cecirse
Raimond, Marie Josephe   11-4-1794
    d/o Jean Raimond & Marie De Barroy
Rasicot
  See: Racicot
Rasicot, Francois   1-23-1800
    s/o Francois Rasicot & Marie Magdeleine Osten dit Marineau
Ravalette, Antoine   7-6-1818
    s/o Louis Ravalette & Agnes Godere
Ravalette, Elizabeth   7-24-1820
    d/o Louis Ravalette & Agnes Goder
Ravalet, Louis   8-2-1784
    s/o Jean Baptiste Ravalet & Josephe Fovel
Ravalet, Louis   10-1-1810
    s/o Louis Ravalet & Agnes Godere
Ravalette, Marguerite   8-16-1802
    d/o Louis Ravalette & Agnes Godere

66

Ravalette, Marie   10-2-1820
    d/o Louis Ravalette & Agnes Godere
Ravalet, Therese   11-11-1813
    d/o Louis Ravalet & Agnes Goder
Reeves, William   6-2-1832
    s/o Gustave Reeves & Lucy Lagin
Renard - Renaud
  See: Delorier - Renault - Deslaurier
Renard dit Deloriers, Marianne   7-3-1820
    d/o Louis Renard dit Deloriers & Marguerite Goder
Renaud dit Deslorier, Geneieve   2-12-1799
    d/o Jean Bte Renaud dit Deslorier & Magdelaine Bordeleau
Renaud, Therese   5-15-1808
    d/o Francois Renaud & Marguerite (Godere)
Renault, Charlotte   10-20-1793
    d/o Charles Renault & Marguerite Lebaux
Renault, Jean Bte   10-26-1750
    s/o Jean B. Renault & Marianne Prevot
Renau dit Delaurier, Pierre   11-11-1813
    s/o Jean Bte Renau dit Delaurier & Magdalene Bordeleau
Rene, Joseph   5-23-1808
    s/o Gabriel Rene & Louise Lapitre
Rene, Joseph Gabriel   6-13-1803
    s/o Gabriel Rene & Louise Oualet
Rene, Louis   7-14-1805
    s/o Amable Rene & Amgdeleine Antailla
Richard, Agnes   8-26-1756
    d/o _____ Richard & Marieanne Le Decouverte
Richard, Jean Baptiste   2-27-1786
    s/o (father unknown) & Magdalene Beausran
Richard, Jean Bte   11-1-1819
    s/o Jean Bte Richard & Elizabeth Mallet
Richard, Marguerite   7-6-1818
    d/o Pierre Richard & Josette St Andre
Richerville, Antoine Drouet de   7-14-1779
    s/o Antoine Drouet de Richerville & Francoise Outlas
Richerville, Jean Baptiste   12-9-1809
    s/o Antoine Richerville & Marie Vaudrie
Richarville, Antoine Drouet de   1-19-1801
    s/o Antoine Drouet de Richarville & Marie Vaudrey
Richerville, Marguerite Drouet de   6-6-1785
    d/o Antoine Drouet de Richerville & Francoise Outlas
Richarville, Marie   9-21-1811
    d/o Antoine Richarville & Marie Vaudri
Richarville, Marie Drouet dit   1-7-1833
    d/o Jean Bte Drouet dit Richarville & Victoire Leveron
Richardville, Michel Drouet de   2-3-1818
    s/o Antoine Drouet de Richardville & Marie Vaudry
Riendeau, Joachim   11-17-1787
    s/o Joachim Rienseau & _____
Rochard, Helene   1-24-1803
    d/o Pierre Rochard & Marie Louise Petit
Rolland, Jacques   2-8-1798
    s/o Claude Rolland & Josette Boursier

Rolus, Samuel   10-1-1810
        s/o Jean Baptiste Rolus & Julienne _____
Roufiance
    See: Laviolette & Roussian
Roussian dit Laviolette, Louis   2-4-1788
        s/o Francois Roussian dit Laviolette & Marie Anne Poineau
Roux, Pierre   1-20-1794
        s/o Pierre Roux & Jeanne Fichere

St Antoine
    See: Vachet
St Antoine, Therese   2-16-1801
        d/o Francois St Antoine & Marie Cardinal
St Aubin, Claude   7-17-1797
        s/o Joseph St Aubin & Julienne Cuiere
St Aubin, Jean Bte   10-19-1760
        s/o Jean Bte St Aubin & Madeleine Pruneau
St Aubin, Louis   4-16-1787
        s/o Jean Bte St Aubin & Marie Louise Denis
St Germaine, Felicite   2-13-1786
        d/o Pierre St Germaine & Felicite Jovillon
St Germaine, Louis H.   10-8-1810
        s/o Antoine St Germain & Marie Charon
St Marie
    See: Racine
St Marie, Francois Racine dit   11-15-1787
        s/o Racine dit St Marie & Anne Du Devoir
St Marie, Joseph   5-22-1785
        s/o Joseph St Marie & Marie Louise Piessalu
St Marie Marie Louise Racine   7-27-1797
        d/o Jean Bte Racine St Marie & Jane Du Devoir
St Martin
    See: Berton
Sanson, Alexander   10-3-1785
        s/o Joseph Sanson & Catherine Picard
Sanson, Victoire   7-6-1818
        d/o Alexander Sanson & Archange Bordeleau
Sans Souci, Joseph   10-1-1810
        s/o Joseph Sans Souci & Geneieve David
Schabart, Joesphe   2-26-1770
        d/o Nicolas Schabart & Marie Claire Stoesher
Sequin dit La Deroute, Barbe   4-24-1792 & %-17-1808
        d/o Alexis Sequin dit La Deroute & Agathe Campaux
Sequin, Cecile   2-10-1800
        d/o Alexis Sequin & Agathe Campeaux
Sequin, Louis   11-23-1818
        s/o Louis Sequin dit Laderout & Marianne Denoyon
Sevigney, Eustache   4-27-1807
        s/o Eustache Sevigny & Marguerite Chevalier
Soudriette, Charles   10-1-1810
        s/o Francis Soudriette & Marguerite Gendron

Souligney, Joseph					1-21-1833
    s/o Eustache Souligney & Marguerite Denoyon
Steward, Marie					1-13-1834
    d/o James Steward & Elizabeth Laplante

Tesie, Francois					6-29-1795
    s/o Pierre Tesie & Geneieve Perant
Tetro, Jean Baptiste				11-28-1787
    s/o Daniel Tetro & Marie Renee Pineau
Theriaque, Michel				1-7-1796
    s/o Francois Theriaque & Magdeleine Menard
Thiere, Maeie Joseph La Tulippe dit		1-21-1788
    d/o Pierre Thiere & Marie Josephe Pelletier
Tierie dit De Frontenac, Pierre		2-4-1788
    s/o Pierre Tiere dit De Fontenac & Marie Josephe Pelletier
Tirio, Anne					2-4-1788
    d/o Jean Chrysostomi Tirio & Julie Campeau
Toiniche, Agathe				2-8-1798
    d/o (Baptiste) Toiniche & Josette
Touga, Auguste					7-16-1801
    s/o Joseph Touga & Jannete Cardinal
Touga, Francois					7-15-1805
    s/o Joseph Augustin Touga & Jeanne Cardinal
Touga, Joseph					4-22-1801
    s/o Joseph Touga & Jeanne Cardinal
Tougas dit Laviolette, Francois		5-6-1833
    s/o Joseph Tougas & Francoise Valee
Tougas, Francois				1-17-1835
    s/o Francois Tougas & Geneieve Vallee
Touga, Guillaume				7-6-1801
    s/o Joseph Touga & Jannete Cardinal
Tougas, Jean Bte				1-18-1773
    s/o Guillaume Tougas & Marianne Quintelle
Tougas, Joseph					1-16-1773
    s/o Guillaume Tougas & Marie Anne Quintale
Toulon, dit Canechou (Ganichou), Jean	12-30-1788
    s/o Jean Toulon & Marie _____
Toulon dit Ganichon, Marie			11-8-1813
    d/o Jean Toulon dit Ganichou & Susanne St Andre
Tremblai, Archange				6-13-1814
    d/o Louis Tremblai & Josette Raimond
Tremblai, Etinne				5-14-1798
    s/o Ambroise Tremblai & Catherine Simar
Trempe dit Cornouailler, Marie Victoire	7-21-1794
    d/o Pierre Trempe dit Cornouailler & Angelique
                            Racine dit Beauchene
Troquier, Francois				7-19-1819
    s/o Francois Troquier & Feleicite Cardinal
Trottier,
    See: Des Riviers
Trottier, Francois				1-2-1792
    s/o Francois Trottier & Louise La Roche

Turpin, Charles   4-8-1833
        s/o Francois Turpin & Josette Gail
Turpin, Francois   7-14-1805
        s/o Francois Turpin & Josephine Levrond
Turpin, Rose   12-19-1809
        d/o Francois Turpin & Marie Josephe Levron

Vachet dit St Antoine, Francois   5-2-1785
        s/o Jean Bte Vachet dit St Antoine & Marie Marguerite
                                                    Pelletier
Vachet, Francois   5-30-1808
        s/o Francois Vachet & Therese Cardinal
Valiquet, Francois   8-2-1784
        s/o Augustien Valiquet & Geneieve Charton
Valle, Alexandre   8-2-1784 & 10-26-1795
        s/o Alexandre Valle & Marie Louise Macou
Valle, Catherine   8-18-1823
        d/o Alexandre Valle & Catherine Langlois
Valle, Francois   10-8-1803
        s/o Alexandre Valle & Francoise Bonneau
Valle, Francoise   4-22-1801
        d/o Alexandre Valle & Francoise Bonneau
Valle, Geneieve   7-15-1805
        d/o Francois Valle & Francoise Bonneau
Valle, Pelagie   5-23-1808
        d/o Alexandre Valle & Francoise Bonneau
Vallet, Victoire   10-19-1818
        d/o Alexandre Vallet & Catherine Langlois
Vaudry, Angelique   11-4-1793
        d/o Antoine Vaudry & Anne Bourasso
Vaudry, Jean Bte   8-26-1756
        s/o Joseph Vaudry & Marie Le Page
Vaudry Jean Bte   6-20-1785
        s/o Jean Bte Vaudrie & Agnes Richard
Vaudrie, Marie   7-14-1779
        d/o Jean Bte Vaudrie & Agnes Richard
Vaudry, Marie Magdeleine   1-3-1757
        d/o Joseph Vaudry & Marie Le Page
Vaudry, Ursule   7-24-1778
        d/o Jean Bte Vaudry & Agnes Richard
Villeneuvem Charles   1-14-1773
        s/o Charles Villeneuve & Marguerite Bernard (Bonneau)
Villeneuve, Charles   3-3-1800
        s/o Charles Villeneuve & Geneieve Bonneau
Villeneuve, Francoise   11-15-1813
        d/o Charles Villeneuve & Geneieve Bonneau
Villeneuve, Geneieve   4-15-1793
        d/o Nicolas Villeneuve (Charles ??) & Geneieve Bonneau
Villeneuve, Joseph   9-20-1802
        s/o Charles Villeneuve & Geneieve Bonneau
Villeneuve, Marguerite   1-19-1801 & 7-14-1805
        d/o Charles Villeneuve & (Marie) Geneieve Bonneau

Villeneuve, Marie   12-19-1809
        d/o Charles Villeneuve & Marie (Geneieve) Bonneau
Violon
   See: Laviolette & Roussian

ST FRANCIS XAVIER CATHOLIC CHURCH

KNOX CO. IND.

DEATH RECORDS

1749 - 1838

BY

BARBARA SCHULL WOLFE
Logansport, Ind.
Feb. 1987

(cross referenced)
c/o child of
d/o daughter of
s/o son of
w/o wife of
h/o husband of
d.　died
b.　born
dit = called
bpt = baptised

Typed By:
ROSALIE LOOKER ROWE

UNKNOWN:

child	d. 9-3-1837
child	bpt 9-29-1802 d. 9-29-1802
	c/o soldier of garrison
-----	Marie age 27 mo. d. 10-15-1797
-----	girl d. 8-19-1792 d/o Joseph-----
-----	Jean Bte age 1 mo. d. 7-10-1789
	c/o soldier of garrison
-----	----- d. 7-10-1779
	by Missionary Priest to the County of the Illinois
-----	d. 10-XX-1767 born in Burgone #270
-----	d. 1763? illegible - Phillbert, Notary #242
-----	Marie d. 1764
-----	-----d. 9-9-1762 #229
foundling,	Elizabeth, bpt 9-6-1787 d. 9-15-1787
-----	Magdelene age 3 mo. d. ¢-3-1789
	d/o Michel (Spaniard) & Elizabeth (English) #127
-----	Emanuel (Spanard) age 30 d. 6-23-1789 Native New Mexico

INDIAN:

-----	d.11-16-1756 woman of St Marie Devernay
Geneieve	3½ yrs. d. 9-27-1802
	d/o Marie, of the tribe Houyas
Marie	age 13 yrs. d. 6-9-1802
	adopted by M.M. widow Tagarouche
Marie	d. 3-20-1802
J. Baptiste	age 15 yrs. d. 12-7-1801
-----	d. 7-13-1801
-----	Houya tribe bpt 8-12-1800 d. 8-12-1800
-----	d. 1-14-1799 c/o savage woman, Josette
	raised by Metayer
3 girls	b.6-6-1799 d. 6-7-1799
	daugs/o savage woman belonging to N. Berthiaume
Bouillon - Dur,	woman d. 11-16-1798 w/o -----Bouillon - Dur
-----	Pascal d. 8-23-1798 "Old Prayer"
	tribe of Pouhoutoutatamy
-----	Francois d. 3-22-1798
	tribe of Houyas band od Lamorre
-----	female d. 11-3-1797
	lived with Ambroise Dagenais
-----	child d. 8-13-1791
	"family of the soldier"
-----	age 4 mo. 8-7-1797
	belonged to Cramaillers
2 children	d/ 12-1-1796 of the nation called Pians
-----	Marie age 10 or 12 yrs. d. 7-28-1796
	of the nation called Pians
-----	Pouhoutatomy d. 7-1-1796
	s/o Great Louis dit "Old Prayer"
de Gonzogus,	Louis d. 7-22-1796 born of savage parents of
	the nation of the Poux
-----	Toiniche d. 5-13-1795 - Poux nation

La Tete, Galee d. 4-26-1796
            nation of the Houyas
Louis dit le Vieux Preant (the old Prayer)   d. 2-16-1796
            Chief - Pouhcutatamy Indians
-----   Joseph d. 1-13-1796   Poux Indian
-----   girl age 4 yrs. d. 2-14-1795
            of Pierre La Forais
Jaques,   1 girl d. 12-7-1793 of Mr. Jaques
De Couere, Francoise age 2 mo. d. 10-15-1793
            d/o De Couere, Chief of the Illinois
-----   girl d. 10-2-1793
            belonging to widow Barrois
-----   girl bapt 6-20-1793 d. 6-21-1793
-----   girl d. 6-16-1793
-----   girl bapt 4-24-1793 d. 4-25-1793
-----   Moutet age 5 yrs. d. 4-1-1793
            living with Mr Renaud
Beauregard "Little Illinois" age 3 yrs. d. 9-13-1837
Constant   (woman) age 35 yrs. d. 3-25-1793 w/o Mr. Constant
-----   Francoise age 40 yrs. d. 1-20-1793
La Bicche   Francois age 26 yrs. d. 10-4-1792
            Chief of the Peoreas
-----   Marguerite bapt. 6-8-1792 d. 6-19-1792
            woman of the Pianquichins
Metayer,   Marie Char age 55 yrs. b. 1734 d. 3-15-1789
            a piankichias - w/o Louis Metayer
Jacques,   Ursule Etinne age 4 yrs. d. 9-21-1788
-----   Francoise age 6 yrs. d. 9-19-1788
            d/o free savage named Fauchon
-----,   Etinne age 6 yrs. d. 9-1-1788 - s/o Jacob-----
-----.   Angelique age 34 yrs. d. 2-22-1809 of the
            Poutiwatimy nation lived with Francois Hameline
-----   d. 12-7-1785 bapt. "Little Savage"
-----   d. 5-3-1786 "Old Savage"
Gritg Nanigou, Catherine age 80 yrs. d. 12-2-1751 Miami Indian
Puducah,   Marie Louise d. 12-16-1751 W/o Joseph------

SLAVES:

-----, Francois   d. 2-10-1756 of Deslauries
-----, Viltoise   d. 11-22-1777 indian woman
Padouca, Charlotte   d. 4-11-1756 legal w/o Padouca slave
                        of Toussaint Lafromboise
-----, Antoine   bapt. 9-13-1787 d. 9-14-1787
                        Piankichias Indian
Cati, Marie   age 70 yrs. d. 4-14-1831
                        negress - w/o M. Catie
-----, Marie Louise   age 2 mo. d. 8-3-1802
                        d/o Rosalie slave of Mr. Cournoyer
-----, Jean Baptiste   age 9 yrs. d. 1-20-1751 - slave of Buttios
-----, Angelique   d. 2-6-1756 slave of Deslauriers
-----, Jean   age 6 days d. 11-19-1786
                        slave of pierre Cournoyer

-----, Gerry or Geneieve d. 4-17-1800 (negress)
                    slave of Laurent Bazadoue
-----, Desire'   d. 6-23-1797 (negress)
                    slave of Francois Lognon
-----, (Negro)   age 50 yrs. d. 3-8-1793 lately baptised -
                    of MMe Droute de Richardville
-----, Cesar   age 64 yrs. d. 2-9-1793 (negro)
                    of Andre St Marie
-----, Francois   (negro) d. 5-8-1792 belonging to
                    Joseph La Motte
-----, (Mulatto)   age 15 yrs. d. 4-19-1791
                    of Pierre Gamelin
-----, (negress)   age 12 yrs. d. 3-24-1791
                    belonging to Francois Bosseron
-----, Thomas   age 30 yrs. d. 9-14-1789 Killed by
                    indians; slave of Sr Bosseron (Negro)
-----, (Negress)   age 4 days d. 10-9-1788
                    slave of Sr Mc Intosh
-----, Sere   (negress) age 90 yrs. d. 9-9-1809
-----, (Negro)   age 4 mo. d. 12-29-1751
                    d/o Alaxander & Dorothee
-----, (Negro)   age 6 mo. d. 10-17-1752
                    d/o Alexandre & Dorothee
-----, Ursule   age 22 days d. 7-8-1787
                    belonging to Pierre Cartier
La Tonton, Marie Francoise d. 8-26-1800 Free Negress

Alard, Louis	d. 10-18-1788 age 5 yrs. 8 mo.
Alard, Victoire	d. 12-4-1790
	d/o Louis Alard & Catherine Lardoise
Alber, ----- Mrs.	d. 1825
Allard, Angelique	d. 10-22-1793 age 3 yrs.
	d/o Louis Allard & Catherine Poitiars
Amelin,-----	d. 3-23-1819
Amelin, Laurent	d. 11-28-1810 age 54 yrs.
Amelin, Marie - See: Cartier, Jean Francois Cartier, Sem	
Amelin, Scolastique	d. 9-8-1801 age 18 mo.
Andrais, Felicite	d. 9-14-1800 age 1 mo.
Andray, (child)	d. 3-3-1799
	c/o Pierre Andray & Josette Boulon
Andray dit Litalien, Joseph	d. 5-30-1801 age 50 yrs. Killed
Andre,(boy)	d. 4-14-1835 s/o Jacques Andre
Andre, (Lady)	d. 1-27-1837 w/o ----- Villeneuve
Andre, Agate see: Delisle (child)	
Andre, Amable	d. 1-11-1835 b. 11-14-1834
	s/o Joseph Andre
Andre, Charles	d. 6-11-1818
	s/o Pierre Andre & Barbe Bonhomme
Andre, Etinne Lajeunesse dit	d. 12-26-1752 age 42
Andre, Geneieve	d. 10-XX-1819 b. 1-8-1819
	d/o Pierre Andre & Geneieve Bonhomme
Andre, Jean	d. 9-24-1837 age 9 mo.
Andre, Jean Marie	d. 2-13-1791 age 6 yrs.
	s/o Joseph Andre & Marie Josephe Du Mais
Andre, Louise	d. 5-7-1838 age 70 yrs.
	w/o Louis Boyer dit Sinnet
Andre, Louise see: Boyer, Ursule	
Andre, Marie	d. 11-11-1789
	d/o Joseph Andre & Marie Josephe Dumais
Andre, Marie	d. 11-11-1790
	d/o Joseph Andre & Marie Josephe Dumais
Andres, Pelegie	d. 5-30-1789 age 2 yrs.
Andres, Pierre see: Bolon, Josette	
Angloise, Magdalene	d. 9-22-1763 w/o ----- Danis
Angloise, Marie	d. 8-26-1788 age 5 yrs.
Arpains see: Turpain	
Arpains (Turpain), Celeste	d. 11-13-1811 age 3 yrs.
	d/o Francois Arpains
Arseneaut dit Durand, Marie Josephe	
	d. 8-24-1785 age 2 yrs.
	d/o John Marie Arseneaut & Catherine Guilbault
Aveline, Elizabeth	d. 10-27-1818 age 3 yrs.
	d/o Francois Avelin & Geneieve Cardinal
Aveline, Marie Elizabeth	d. 2-21-1812 age 2 yrs.
Baiargeon, Victoire	d. 2-20-1793 age 8 mo.
	d/o Nicolas Baiargeon & Francoise Flichon
Billargeon, Eustache	d. 9-17-1788 age 7½ mo.
Baillargeon, Pierre	d. 9-24-1821 age 15 mo.
Ballargeon, Nicolas	d. 5-5-1803
Barbau, Francois see: Deganne, Archange	

Barbeau, Francois	d. 8-1-1835 age 70 yrs.
	h/o late Archange Laforet
Barcellon, Rose	d. 1-6-1821
Barnabe, Charles Jean	d. _____
	s/o Antoine Barnabe & Marie Laviolette
Baron, Toussaint	d. 10-2-1789
	s/o Francois Baron & Suzanne Racine
Baronet, Alexis	d. 1-1-1793 age 26 yrs.
Baroy, Lambert see: Danis, Marie Louise	
Baroy, Leon	d. 11-15-1810 age 34 yrs.
Barril, Francois	d. 10-16-1797
Barrois,(boy)	6-30-1835 age 2 yrs.
	s/o Jean Marie Barrois
Barrois, (girl)	d. 3-6-1838
Barrois, Catherine(Miss)	d. 4-30-1838
Barrois, Francois	d. 12-24-1803 b. 1779 age 24 yrs.
Barrois, J.M.	d. 12-10-1836 uncle of Lambert (Barrois)?
Barrois, Lamber (Charles)	d. 12-10-1837 b. 1767 age 70 yrs.
Barrois, Lambert see: Bono, Angelique	
Barrois, Louis	d. 9-17-1788 age 4 yrs. 8 mo.
Barrois, Pierre	d. 12-11-1803 age 1 mo.
	s/o Joseph Barrois
Barrois - Barrouet, M^Me - miacarriage 2-25-1793 widow of	
	Francois Barrouet (from Small Pox)
Barrouet - Baroy - Barroia, Francois	d. 1-2-1793 age 30 yrs.
	h/o Jeanne Racine?
Barron, Cecile (indian)	d. 5-14-1801 w/o Joseph Barron
Barron, Francios	d. 2-13-1795 age 61 yrs.
Barron, Joseph	d. 1-18-1803 age 3 mo.
Barron, Marie Anne	d. 10-2-1808 age 19 mo.
	d/o Joseph Barron &
	Barbe Brouillet (d. before 5-1-1808)
Barsalous, Jeannette	d. 2-18-1795 age 25 yrs.
Baulon, Gabriel	d. 6-21-1813 age 37 yrs.
Baunau, Jean Baptiate	d. 1-28-1813 age 56 yrs.
Bautin, Joseph	d. 2-1-1769 age 55 yrs. (bachelor)
Bautron, Marie Angelique see: Mallet, (boy)	
Bayargeon,-----	d. 10-15-1797 age 3 or 4 yrs.
Bayjenly or Boyenly see: La de Boyenly	
Bazinet, Francois	d. 11-24-1786 b. 1750 age 36 yrs.
Beaulieu, Francois Rasine	d. 1-29-1764
Beaulon, Geneieve	d. 9-2-1788 age 4 yrs. d/o Amable Beaulon
Beauregard, Jeane	d. 3-18-1836 age old
Belange, Simon	d. 11-19-1811 age 33 yrs.
Belay, Jean see: Vacher, Marie	
Belon see: Lefevre	
Belorny see: Leuvar	
Benac,-----	d. 3-24-1837 age 20 yrs. w/o Charles Metay
Benoit, Joseph	d. 9-27-1794 age 17 mo. 3 days
Bergan, Dominique dit Jean lours age 48 yrs.	
	d. Grand Rapids on the Wabash
	buried 9-8-1787
Bergan, Marguerite	d. 8-26-1788 age 2 mo.
Bergan, Marie Victoire	d. 12-10-1788 age 11 days
Bergan, (child)	d. 10-30-1838

Bergeron, Louis   d. 5-19-1797
Berton, Etienne Martin   d. 4-16-1770
Beutron dit Major, Angelique see: Mallet, Marie
Bigalion, Benois   d. 1-9-1814 age 2 yrs. 3 mo.
Binet, Francoise   d. 6-11-1786 age 1 mo. 6 days
Binet, Toussaint   d. 12-26-1790
                         s/o Jean Bte Binet & Madeleine La Costa
Binette, Jean Baptiste   d. 1-2-1791 age 18 yrs.
                         s/o Jean Bte Binette & Madeleine La Costa
Bishop, Elizabeth   d. 10-23-1838 w/o Vital Boucher
Bissaillion, Francois B. d. 10-16-1810
Bissaillion, Etienne   d. 8-11-1821 age 60 yrs.
Bissonet, Joseph   d. 9-7-1758
                         s/o Joseph Bissonet & Marguerite Castangue
Bizazon, Bernice see: Picard, Pierre Francois
Board, Francis   d. 8-25-1835 age 2 yrs.
Bolon, Amable   d. 7-XX-1823
Bolon, Antoine   d. 7-22-1809 age 20 yrs.
Bolon, Josette   d. 9-28-1810 age 30 yrs.
                         d/o Pierre Andre
Boneau,-----   d. 2-25-1793 b. 2-25-1793
                         c/o MMe Pierre Bono
Boneau, J.B. see: Pakans, Marie
Boneau, Josephe see: Brouillet, Francois - Brouyette, Francois
Bonhomme, Barbe see: Andre, Charles
Bonhomme, Geneieve see: Andre, Geneieve
Bonhomme, Geneieve see: Hunaux, Joseph
Bonhomme, Marianne   d. 11-12-1832 age 28 yrs.
                         w/o Jean Baptiste Richardville Jr.
Bonneau, Anne   d. 12-27-1790
                         d/o Pierre Bonneau & Anne Cournoyer
Bonneau, Barbe see: Brouzet (girl)
Bonneau, Claude   d. 1-28-1764 b. 1-18-1764
Bonneau, Fortunes   d. 5-20-1798 age 1 mo.
Bonneau, Francoise   d. 1-12-1793 b. 2-12-1765 age 28 yrs.
                         w/o Alexandre Valiere - Valle - La Valle
Bonneau, Geneieve   d. 4-24-1799 age 5 or 6 yrs.
Bonneau, Jannete   d. 11-15-1800 w/o Toussaint Dubois
Bonneau, Josette see: Brouzette, Francois
Bonneau, Michael Charles d. 1-29-1764 b. 1-18-1764
Bonneau, Tharese   d. 9-28-1788 age 5 yrs.
Bono, Angelique   d. 10-17-1837 age 71 yrs.
                         w/o Lambert Barrois
Bono, Francois   d. 4-30-1831 age 45 yrs.
                         widower of Francoise Ravalet
Bono, Jeanne see: Soligne, Bridgette
Bono, Marie   d. 9-21-1831 age 45 yrs.
                         w/o Francois Godaire
Bono, Pierre see: Cournoyer, Helene
Bonscouyon see: La Feuillade
Bontin, Francois   d. 7-22-1802 bpt. 3-20-1802
Bordelau, Lasalle see: Languedoc, Elizabeth
Bordelau, Magdeleine   d. 2-22-1819 age 55 yrs.
                         w/o Jean Bte Deslorier

Bordeleau, (girl)	d. 3-29-1803 b. 3-29-1803 d/o Michel Bordeleau
Bordeleau, Antoine	d. 10-29-1793 age 68 yrs. h/o Catherine Caron
Bordeleau, Bridgette	d. 10-6-1831 age 1 yr. 3 days d/o Michel Bordeleau & Angelique Cournoyer
Bordeleau, Catherine	see: Mallet, Marguerite
Bordeleau, Charles	d. 5-27-1789 age 18 yrs. died of wounds from indians
Bordeleau, Francoise	d. 7-24-1790 age 1½ yrs.
Bordeleau, Magdeleine	see: Renaud dit Desloriers, Vicroire
Bordeleau, Marc	d. 10-25-1803 s/o Michel Bordeleau
Bordeleau, Susanne	d. 4-28-1831 d/o Pierre Bordeleau & Ester Valet
Bordeleau, Ursule	d. 11-23-1810 age 21 yrs.
Bosseron, Francois	d. 8-16-1791 age 40 yrs.
Botler, Marie	d. 6-29-1833 w/o Jacques Botler (negro)
Boucher, Celeste	see: Generaux, Francois
Boucher, Francois	see: Fontenay, Marie
Boucher, Guillaume	d. 9-27-1831 b. 4-9-1831 s/o Francois Boucher & Marie Dequinte
Boucher, Jean Bte	see: Cartier, Elizabeth
Boucher, Julie	see: Brouillet, (boy)
Boucher, Marie	d. 4-4-1837 age 9 yrs. D/o Amable Boucher
Boucher, Marie Elise	d. 9-24-1820 age 9 mo. d/o Vitel Boucher & Odelle Brouillete
Boucher, Vital	d. 10-23-1838 see: Bishop, Elizabeth
Boucher, Vital	see: Cardinal, Marie Josephe
Bouissard	see: Ravalet
Boulon, (girl)	d. 1-1-1796 d/o Amable Boulon & Josette Godere
Boulon, Josette	see: Andray, (child)
Boulon, Louis	d. 6-21-1799
Bourdeleau	see: Lamy
Bourdeleau, Pierre Lami dit	see: Valet, Ester
Boutin, -----	See: Dany
Boyer, (child)	d. 3-12-1795 age 8 mo. c/o Louis Boyer
Boyer, (girl)	d. 11-8-1790 d/o Louis Courtaux dit Boyer
Boyer, (male)	d. 12-9-1838 drowned in Wabash
Boyer, Charles	d. 4-1-1803 age 2½ yrs. s/o Francois Boyer & Barbe Sequin
Boyer, Charlotte	see: La Chine Du Devoir, (child)
Boyer, Francois	d. 1-27-1835
Boyer, Francoise	d. 8-12-1786 age 14½ yrs.
Boyer, Francoise	see: Laderoute, Marie Elizabeth
Boyer, Jean Baptiste	d. 10-11-1797 age 14 mo.
Boyer, Louis	see: Mete, Catherine
Boyer, Louis	d. 3-12-1795 age 8 mo.
Boyer, Sr Louis	d. 8-8-1786 Teree Haute, on Wabash age 59 yrs.
Boyer dit Courteau, Louis	see: Lapointe, Catherine
Boyer dit Sinnet, Louis	see: Andre, Louise
Boyer, Marie	d. 5-30-1793 Kaskias age 65 yrs.
Boyer, Marie	d. 2-9-1793 age 2 mo. d/o Francois Boyer & Barbe Saquien

Boyer, Marie	d. 1-30-1837 w/o Joseph Grimard
Boyer, Marie Louise	d. 7-26-1820 age 66 yrs. w/o Charles Dudevoir
Boyer, Pierre	d. 8-10-1802 age 17 mo.
Boyer, Ursule	d. 12-1-1794 age 1 yrs. d/o Toussaint Boyer & Louise Andre
Bradly, Guillaume Marie	d. 10-27-1821 age 9 mo.
Brady,-----	d. 9-3-1814 age 2 yrs.
Breaden, Rosan	d. 9-26-1802 American widow
Bredy, Catherine	d. 4-20-1819 age 3 yrs. d/o John Bredy & Peggy Hecthrop
Brisard, (child)	d. 9-23-1838 d/o Mr. Brisard of Faux-Chennel
Brossard, Joseph	d. 5-14-1789 killed by indians age 42
Bouett, Michel see: Richardville, Marie Louise	
Brouillet, (child)	d. 5-30-1835 c/o Pierre Brouillet
Brouillet, (girl)	d. 2-23-1837 age 12 yrs. d/o Pierre Brouillet
Brouillet, (boy)	d. 3-11-1819 b. 3-11-1819 s/o Pierre Brouillet & Julie Boucher
Brouillet, Barbe	d. before 5-1-1808 see: Barron, Marie Anne
Brouillet, Caroline	d. 4-4-1820 b. 3-23-1820
Brouillet, Elizabeth	d. 10-8-1802 w/o -------- Brouillet
Brouillet, Elizabeth	d. 9-28-1808 age 1 yr. d/o Michel Brouillat & Marie Richerville
Brouillet, Etienne	d. 9-4-1788 age 4 mo.
Brouillet, Francoise	d. 4-22-1793 age 3 yrs. d/o Francois Brouillet & M. Josephe Boneau
Brouillet, Marie Louise	d. 9-4-1787 age 3 yrs. d/o Louis Brouillet & Marie Louise Desnoyers
Brouillet, Michel	d. 12-27-1838
Brouillet, Michel	d. 1-5-1797
Brouillet, Ursule	d. 11-14-1788
Brouillete, Odelle see: Boucher, Marie Elise	
Brouzet, (girl)	d. 1-14-1792 d/o Michel Brouzet & Barbe Bonneau
Brouzette, Benite	d. 11-15-1811 age 25 yrs.
Brouzette, Etsidor	d. 10-7-1790 s/o Louis Brouzette & Louise Denoye
Brouzette, Francois	d. 1-4-1791 age 6 yrs. s/o Francois Brouzette & Josette Bonneau
Brouzette, Francois	d. 1-20-1791 s/o Louis Brouzette & Louise Denoye
Brown, (boy)	d. 2-19-1835 s/o Andre Brown of Edgar Co. Ill.
Brown, (boy)	d. 7-20-1837 age 3 mo.
Butler see: Botler	
Butter, (girl)	d. 2-7-1838 age 26 yrs.
Buvinet, ----- see: Tierry, Pierre	
Cabascier, Marie Louise see: Cartier, Louson	
Cabassier, Bridgette	d. 11-6-1800 age 14 mo.
Cabassier, Pierre	d. 5-6-1809 age 61 yrs.
Cabassier, (boy)	d. 3-20-1820 b. 3-19-1820 s/o Victoire Cabassier

Cadoret, Francois see: Godere, Marie
Cadoret, M.   d. 3-11-1835
Campnotte, Isaac   d. 6-25-1809 b. 2-7-1799 age 13 yrs.
Campan, Michel   d. 9-9-1823
Campau, Jeanne   d. 7-31-1835 age 50 yrs.
                           w/o Sem La Rocher
Campeau, Agate   d. 1-8-1790 age 50 yrs.
                           2nd husband - Andre Landaus
Campeau, Helen see: Ravalet, Isamel - Ravalet, Michel
Campeau, Marie Jeanne see: Racuse, Francois
Campo, Susanne   d. 12-7-1820 age 2 yrs.
Caniolets, Alexis   d. 3-12-1795 age 68 yrs.
Cara, Antoine   d. 8-26-1788 age 9 mo.
Cardinal, Barbe see: Pelletier, Geneieve
Cardinal, Cecile see: Metayer dit Leveron, (girl)
                     Metayer dit Leveron, Joseph
Cardinal, Celete   d. 11-5-1801 age - a few days
Cardinal, Constant see: Coderette Marguerite
Cardinal, Felicite see: Trochet, (girl)
Cardinal, Geneieve see: Avelin, Elizabeth
Cardinal, Henriette see: Lognon, Louis
Cardinal, Jacques   d. 10-20-1810 age 45 yrs.
Cardinal, Jean   d. 8-23-1835 age 11 yrs.
Cardinal, Jean Bte   d. 5-5-1820 age 35 yrs.
Cardinal, Jeanne see: Tougas, Isaac - Tougas, Leonard
Cardinal, Joseph   d. 1-28-1832 age 1 mo. 20 days
                           s/o Joseph Cardinal Jr.
Cardinal, Julie see: Languedoc, Joseph
Cardinal, Louis   d. 12-30-1790
                           s/o Jacques Cardinal & Barbe Deligne
Cardinal, Marianne see: Compagnote, Antoine
Cardinal, Marie see: Compagnot, Antoine
Cardinal, Marie Josephe   d. 4-28-1838 age 75 yrs.
                           w/o Vital Boucher
Cardinal, Nicolas   d. 8-23-1789 age 60 yrs.
Cardinal, Rosanna   d. 10-5-1838 at Mr. Stouts
Cardinal dit Lajeoze, Toussaint d. 2-26-1793
                           s/o Nicolas Cardinal (deceased) &
                           Marie Girard
Carie, Alexis see: St Amand, Marie Madeleine
Carie, Francois see: Dubois, Louise
Caron, Catherine see: Bordeleau, Antoine
Carpentier, Jean Baptiste d. 9-10-1791 age 55 yrs.
Carpentier, Dme Pelagie   d. 6-29-1789 age 36 yrs.
                           w/o Charles Vlle (Valle)
Carqueix, Helene   d. 1-20-1804 age 60 yrs.
Carretier, Theresa   d. 2-8-1821 age 8 days
Carroll, (child)   d. 9-4-1837 age 6 mo.
Carroll, (girl)   d. 9-28-1838
Carroll, Jeannette Marie see: Tabba, Charles
Carron, Marie Louise   d. 1-14-1802
                           widow of Antoine Lefevre dit Chapeau

Carter, Jean   d. 8-15-1802 (Irishman) age 55 yrs.
Cartier, Ambrois see: Laforet, Julie
Cartier, Antoine see: Mallet, Francois
Cartier, Marie Elizabeth d. 9-4-1813 w/o Jean Bte Boucher
Cartier, Francois   d. 9-14-1821 age 2 yrs. 7 mo.
Cartier, Heleine   d. 8-12-1789 age 9 yrs.
Cartier, Jean Francois   d. 1-26-1832 age 9 mo.
            s/o Joseph Cartier & Marie Amelin
Cartier, Louison   d. 8-27-1831 age 3 mo.
            s/o Louison Cartier & Marie Louise Cabascier
Cartier, Pierre   d. 8-8-1837 age 21 yrs.
Cartier, Sem   d. 9-3-1835
            s/o Joseph Cartier & Marie Amelin
Cartier, Susanne   d. 7-22-1835 age 32 yrs.
            w/o Robert Russell
Cartier, Victoire   d. 5-24-1821 age 21 yrs.
Castangue, Marguerite see: Bissonet, Joseph
Cati, Isabella   d. 8-18-1835 age 5 yrs.
Catis, Antoine   d. 12-13-1795 age 6 or 7 yrs.
            s/o Joseph Catis & --------------
Caty, Antoine   d. 11-16-1798 age 40 yrs.
Caudere, Louis   d. 6-15-1791 age 43 yrs.
Chabutte, Joseph   d. 5-29-1791 age 43 yrs. killed by indians
Chabolle, Joseph see: Clermont, Ursule
Chabot, Louis   d. 9-16-1788 age 1 yrs. 16 days
Charbotborn, Louis   d. 7-27-1786 bpt 7-27-1786
Chambeau, Antoine   d. 10-5-1787 age 25 yrs.
Chapart, Barbe   d. 12-3-1801 age 17 yrs.
Chapart, Joseph   d. 12-18-1809 bpt 5-14-1790 age 16 yrs.
Chapart, Nicolas   d. 10-12-1800
Chapeaux, see: Lefevre
Chappard, Jacques   d. 2-24-1793 b. 1-1-1793 age 2 mo.
            s/o Nicolas Chappard & Cecile Lamote
Chappart, Marie   d. 2-21-1835 at Riviere Au Chat
Chappert, (boy)   d. 12-16-1750 s/o Nicolas Chappert
Charlemagne, Pierre   d. 8-17-1808 age 2½ yrs.
Charpunaux, Jean Bte   d. 2-22-1794 age 70 Yrs.
Chartier see: Garretier
Chartier, Celeste   d. 8-1-1788 b. 6-13-1783 age 5 yrs.
            d/o Joseph Chartier   (receipts)
Chartier, Joseph   d. 4-20-1809 age 58 yrs.
Chartier, Joseph see: Renaud, Charlotte
Chartier, Marie Louise   d. 2-25-1793 age 40 yrs.
Chartier, Michel   d. 2-20-1793 age 15½ yrs.
            s/o Joseph Chartier & Marie Louise -----
Chatigney, (boy)   d. 10-8-1792 age 18 mo.
            s/o Ignace Chatigney & -------
Chenet, Felix   d. 3-12-1838 age 21 yrs.
Chevalier, w. (male)   d. 10-30-1798
Clairmont, Elizabeth see: Dielle (girl)
Clairmont, Marguerite see: Range, Marguerite
Clark, Guillaume   d. 11-12-1802
            Judge of Supreme Court of Indiana territory
Clements, M. see: Mahoney

Clermont, Ursule   d. 10-12-1790 age 40 yrs.
                         w/o Joseph Chabolle
Coderitte, Marguerite   d. 8-23-1835 age 3 yrs.
                         d/o Louis Coderitte & Constant Cardinal
Codere, Pierre   d. 5-24-1789 killed by indians age 53 yrs.
Collens, Etienne   d. 9-19-1819 age 50 yrs.
Compagnot, Adelaide see; Racine Nos
Compagnot, Antoine   d. 2-5-1793 b. 4-14-1789 age 4 yrs.
                         s/o Francois Compagnot & Marie Cardinal
Compagnot, Marianne   d. 11-19-1801 widow age 82 yrs.
Compagnot, Therese   d. 10-10-1803
                         w/o Francois Languedoc
Compagnot, Pierre   age 50 yrs. ??
Compagnote, Antoine   d. 1-18-1795 age 10 yrs.
                         s/o Francois Compagnote & Marianne Cardinal
Compagnotte, Therese see: Languedoc, Pierre
Compot, Catherine see: Gaudere, Rene
Conisant see: Duchene
Conover, (child)   d. 7-5-1837 age 3 mo.
Constant, Elizabeth   d. 10-12-1795 age 5 yrs.
Cornoilier, Angelique see: Denoyan, Louis
Cornoiller, Antoine   d. 11-2-1831 age 11 yrs.
                         s/o Antoine Cornoiller & Therese Germain
Cornoiller, Claude   d. 11-15-1834(small pox) age 18 yrs.
                         s/o Antoine Cornoiller & Therse Germain
Cornoualie see: Trampe
Cornoyer, Marie Geneieve d. 8-18-1832 age 2 yrs.
                         d/o Pierre Cornoyer &---------------
Cornoyer, Pierre   d. 8-16-1821 age 2 yrs.
Coupin, Antoine Claude Gabriel d.7-7-1802 age 33 yrs.
Cournoyer, Angelique see: Bordeleau, Bridget
Cournoyer, Anne see: Bonneau, Anne
Cournoyer, Helene   d. 5-3-1833 age 65 yrs.
                         w/o late Pierre Bono
Cournoyer, Marguerite   d. 7-26-1835 age 3 yrs.
                         d/o Pierre Cournoyer
Courteau, see: Boyer
Craily, Jerome   d. 5-8-1821 age 18 yrs.
Crepau, Catherine see: Tougas dit La Violette, Louis
Crepau, Catherine see: Touga, Therese
Crely, Antoine   d. 5-1-1803 age 20 yrs.
Crepon, Louise see: mallet, Joseph
Cuddy, Ann   d. 8-21-1832 age 46 yrs.
Custas, Josephe   d. 10-30-1777
                         w/o Sr Andre le Costa dit Languedoc
Custeaud, Jean Bte   d. 8-12-1803 age 1 mo.

Dagenais,-----   d. 11-20-1797 b. 11-19-1797
                         c/o Ambroise Dagenais & savage woman
Dagenais see: Outlas, Francoise
Daganux de Guindre,----- d. 6-13-1799
Dagneau, Angelique see: Delisle, Josette

```
Dagneau, Geneieve          d. 3-14-1796 b. 3-14-1796
Dagneau, Jean Bte          d. 3-16-1796 b. 3-14-1796
D'Albee, Helen             d. 11-9-1832 age 11 mo. 10 days
                           d/o Antoine D'Albee & Marie Villeneuve
Danis, Antoine             d. 7-31-1792 age 36 yrs.
Danis,----- see: Angloise, Magdelene
Danie, Honore              d. 10-22-1792 age 50 yrs.
Danis, Marie Louise        d. 8-3-1792 age 22 yrs
                           w/o Lambert Baroy
Dany, Hore see: Godere, Marie Josephe
Dany, Antoine see: Wau, Marie Joseph
Dany dit Boutin, Antoine   d. 6-23-1794 age 3 yrs.
Dany - Danis, (boy)        d. 8-18-1792
                           s/o Antoine Dany & -----Gauder
Daperon, Louis             d. 9-15-1787 b. 3-4-1787 age 6 mo.
Dapron, Giollaume          d. 6-21-1813 b. 5-12-1770 age 46 yrs.
Dapron, Gillaume see: Fausement?, Susan Therese
Darby, Antoine             d. 2-XX-1836
Dardenne, Isabelle alzire  d. 9-23-1832 age 4½ mo.
Dargiulleur see: Derguilleur
David,-----                d. 9-28-1820 age 20 yrs. (Englishman)
DeGane, Magdeleine         d. 11-8-1798 w/o Joseph DeGane
DeGane or DeCane, Marianne d. 12-13-1803
DeGane, Joseph see: Ravalette, Magdelaine
Deganne, Archange          d. 1-22-1820 w/o Francois Barbau
DeGane, Joseph see: Prudomme, Madeleine
De Garde, Elizabeth        d. 7-1-1821 age 20 mo.
Deguele, Susanne see: Lagarde, Dominique
Dejean, Antoinette         d. 9-21-1795 age 2 or 3 mo.
Dejean, Eleanor            d. 7-26-1835 age 2 yrs.
                           d/o Alexis Dejean & Eleanor Villenauve
Dejean, Marie              d. 12-6-1834 age 80 yrs.
                           w/o M. Dejean - who left here 12 yrs.
                           ago - lives near Detroit -
                           M/o Richard Goyaux
Dejean, -----Mrs.          d. 11-12-1838
Deligne, -----Mrs.         d. 1825 w/o Joseph Deligne ?
Deligne, (child)           d. 10-4-1838
Deligne, Barbe see: Cardinal, Louis
Deligne, Francoise         d. 12-28-1832 w/o Peter Godaire
Delile, Amable             d. 2-8-1793 age 54 yrs.
Delile, Amable see: Meloche, Marie Josephe
Delile, Charles see: Barsalous, Jeanette
De Lile, Francoise         d. 2-27-1793 age 2 yrs.
                           d/o Amable Delile (deceased) &
                           Marie Meloche (deceased)
Delille, Jean              d. 8-17-1835 age 2 yrs.
                           d/o Noel Delille & Jenny Ferris (protestant)
Delille, Josette see: Joyeuse, Pierre
Delilles, Charles Mr.      d. 11-22-1838
Deline, (child)            d. 10-6-1838
Delisle, (child)           d. 1-14-1801
                           d/o Charles Delisle & Agathe Andre
Delisle, Cecille see: Edeline, Joseph
```

Delisle, Jean see: Valle, Victoire
Delisle, Josette   d. 9-12-1831 age 21 mo.
                          d/o Charles Delisle & Angelique Dagneau
Delaurier, Marguerite   d. 2-6-1825
Delorier, -----   d. 1-15-1836 age 50 yrs.
Delorier, Francoise see: Languedoc - Langdot, Mrs. Elizabeth
                         Vachette, Louis
Delorier, Xavier see: St Marie, Cecile
Denaud, Francois   d. 8-9-1801 age 6 mo.
Deniau, Pierre   d. 2-16-1793 b. 1736 age 57 yrs.
Denis, Jacques   d. 2-4-1802 age 54 yrs.
Denos, P.   d. 1-19-1838 age 6 yrs.
Denoyan, Louis   d. 11-15-1785
                          h/o Marie Anne Pallu
Denoyan, Louis   d. 8-3-1835 age 60 yrs.
                          h/o Angelique Cornoilier
Denoyan, Marie Anne   d. 1-19-1809 age 30 yrs.
Denoyans, Angelique   d. 10-25-1811 age 38 yrs.   Cornoiler ??
Dequinte, Marie see: Boucher, Guillaume
Derquilleur, Jean Pierre d. 7-22-1796
                          buried Fort Massac on the Ohio
Derosier, Francois   d. 11-18-1810 age 19 yrs.
Derosiers,----- see: Latrimonille, Francois
Derosiers, Antoine   d. 9-7-1788 age 19 mo.
Derousse see : Guerosse
Derousse, Heleine   d. 2-12-1786 age 5 yrs.
Descarraux see: Room
Descouteaux, Joseph   d. 4-5-1799
Desjardens, Hiacynthe see: Page, Madeleine
Des Lauriers see: Renaud
Deslauriers, Antoine   d. 10-30-1838 age 22 yrs.
Deslauriers, Arcangelle Renaud d. 2-11-1793
Des Lauriers, Francoise d. 1-19-1793 age 1yr.
Deslauriers, Jean Bte Renaud d. 6-2-1789 age 3 yrs.
Deslauriers, Joseph see: Lafuirse - Cheniere, Elizabeth
Deslauriers, Marguerite Renaud d. 4-14-1787 age 2 mo.
Desloge, (widow)   d. 11-14-1818
Deslorier, J.B. see: Bordelau, Magdeleine
Deslorier, Pierre   d. 1-18-1819 age 2½ yrs.
                          s/o Pierre Deslorier & Clothide Lavalette
Desloriez, Francois   d. 11-22-1800 age 2 yrs.
Desnoyer, Francoise see: Godere, (girl)
Desnoyer, Louise see: Brouillet, Marie Louise
                         Brouyette, Estiedor
                         Brouyette, Francois
Despointes, Geneieve   d. 11-30-1786 age 55 yrs.
                          w/o Joseph Maisonville
Desriviers, Julien   d. 1-15-1751 age 2 mo.
                          s/o Julien Desriviers & Josette Marie
Desrosiers de Tremble, Bonaventure see: Durivage , Marguerite
Desrosiers, Eulalie   d. 8-28-1788 age 8 yrs. 9 mo.
                          d/o Bonaventure Desrosiers &
                          Marie Louise Lefeure
Desrosiers, Nicolas   d. 3-9-1789 age 2 days

Desrozier, Bonaventure   d. 4-15-1802
Des Ruisseaux, Sieur Paul   d. 7-26-1786 age 40 yrs. (gun shot)
Detalien, Agate see: Charlemagne, Pierre
Devegnet, Marie   d. 9-28-1790 age 57 yrs.
    w/o Jean Marie Philippe Le Gras
Dielle, (girl)   d. 1-15-1792 d/o Francois Dielle &
    Elizabeth Clairmont
Dielle see: Guiele
Dielle, Louis   d. 11-29-1790 age 6yrs.
Dintelmozar, David   d. 10-5-1833 age 56
    of Wurdenberg, Germany
Dizi or Oizi, Michel see: Du Devoir, Barbe
Domean, Alexis dit La Guerre d. 12-12-1755
Donavan, -----Miss   d. 1-21-1838 age 13 yrs.
Du Be, Marie Joseph   d. 9-25-1786 age 5 yrs.
Dubois,----- see: Morel, Jean Bte
Dubois, Charles   d. 11-22-1819 age 24 yrs.
Dubois, Elizabeth   d. 12-11-1835 age 8 mo.
    d/o Jean Bte Dubois & Marie Langlois
Dubois, Francois   d. 10-12-1794 age 3 days
Dubois, Jean Bte   d. 11-29-1801
Dubois, Jean Bte see: La Belle, Euphrasie
Dubois, Joseph   d. 5-10-1799 age 18 mo.
Dubois, Joseph   d. 5-30-1812 b. 1762 age 50 yrs.
Dubois, Louise   d. 9-1-1790 age 40 yrs.
    w/o Francois Carie
Dubois, Marie   d. 12-19 1819 few mo. old d/o Charlotte Dubois
Dubois, Nicolas   d. 6-13-1800
Dubois, Odelle   d. 11-11-1811 age 11 yrs.
    d/o Joseph Dubois
Dubois, Pierre   d. 11-4-1788 age 9 mo.
Dubois, Suzanne see: Jones, William
Duboise, Toussaint   d. 3-1-1816 drowned
Dubois, Toussaint see: Bonneau, Jannet
Dubroil, Charlotte see: La Plante, Josep
Duchaine dit Consiant, Marie 12-31-1794 age 7 yrs.
    d/o Jean Bte Duchaine & Charlotte Ouelete
Ducharme,----- se: Renaud, Charlotte
Ducharmes, Joseph   d. 2-11-1793 age 72 yrs.
Duchene, (child)   d. 9-13-1838 c/o Toussaint Duchene
Duchene, Helene   d. 11-9-1800 age 6 or 7 mo.
Duchene dit Consiant, J.B. see: Qualette, Charlotte
Duchene dit Conisant, Jean Bte d. 12-8-1803
Duchene, Silvestre   d. 11-6-1800 age 40 yrs.
Duchene, Toussaint   d. 11-30-1838
Dudevoir see: La Chine
Ducro dit Laterhem - or Laterreur, Jacques d. 11-1-1777
Du Devoir, Barbe   d. 3-8-1789 age 69 yrs.
    w/o late Michel Dizi or Oizi
Du Devoir, Charles   d. 1-31-1793 age 57 yrs.
Dudevoir, Charles see: Boyer, Marie Louise
Du Devoir dit La Chine, Jean Bte d. 9-11-1786 age 5 yrs.
Du Dvoir, Nicolas   d. 6-19-1788 age 7 mo.
Dugal, Antoine   d. 12-1-1788

Du Mais, Marie Josephe   see: Andre, Jean Marie - Andre, Marie
Dupre, Eloise   d. 11-31-1831 age 4 mo.
                          d/o Louis Dupre & Francoise Gonzales
Dupres, Elizabeth   d. 10-27-1802 age 11 mo.
Durand   see: Arsenaut
Durand dit Montimirel, Joseph d. 12-13-1784 age 6 days
                          bpt. 12-12-1784
Durivage, Marguerite   d. 12-16-1750
                          d/o Bonaventure Desrosiers de Tremble
Durivage, Marguerite   see: Du Tremble, Julian
Dutour, Pierre   d. 10-13-1788 age 35 yrs.
                          s/o Pierre dutour & Magdeleine Montplasier
Dutramble, Felecite   d. 2-25-1793 age 2 mo.
                          d/o Bonaventure Dutramble &
                          Marie Louise Lefevre
Dutramble dit segaud Le Fleur, Louis   d. 9-27-1794 age 50 yrs.
                          killed by indians
Dutremble, Julien   d. 1-4-1751 b. 12-16-1750
                          s/o Bonaventure Tremble &
                          Marguerite Durivage
Dutremble, Marie   d. 2-22-1793 age 17 yrs.

Ebert, Louis   d. 12-13-1811 age 30 Yrs.
Edeline, Andre   d. 12-16-1803 bpt 12-10-1803
Edeline, Barbe   d. 8-20-1799 age 6½ mo.
Edeline, Joseph   d. 3-17-1819 h/o Cecille Delisle
Edeline, Louis   d. 4-28-1799 "Judge of the peace"
Edeline, Louis   d. 10-1-1802 age 2½ to 3 yrs.
Edeline, Marie   d. 5-21-1796 (decending the Wabash)
                          w/o Colonel Hamtramck
Edeline, Marie   see: Hamtramck, Henriette
Edeline, Nicolas   d. 11-23-1800 age 3 mo.
Edeline, Victoire   d. 10-15-1798 age 25 mo.
                          d/o Nicolas Edeline & Therese Godere
Ejould   see: Rarinseau
Escortain - Escort, Jean Bte   d. 10-11-1752 age 30 yrs.

Faubert, Pierre   d. 12-18-1803 age 20 yrs.
Faucher, Bonaventure   d. 6-18-1798 (of the bloody flux)
Fauchoir?, Marie   9-28-1790 age 2 yrs.
Fausement?, Susan Therese   d. 5-10-1820
                          w/o 1) Jean Toulon dit Ganichow
                              2) Guillaume Dapron
Fausement, Susanne   see: Toulon, Susanne
Ferris, Jenny   see: Delille, Jean
Flichon, Francoise   see: Baiargeon, Victoire
Foco, Jeann   see; Leonardy, Pierre
Fontenai, Marguerite   d. 6-6-1797 age 6 mo.
Fontenay, Francois   d. 4-5-1801 age 3 mo.
Fontenay, Jean Bte   d. 7-23-1799 age 8 days
Fontenay, Marie   d. 9-18-1831 b. 1795 age 26 yrs.
                          w/o Francois Boucher

Frazer, Francis	d. 1-11-1837 age 8 yrs.
Frazer, Mrs.	d. 3-27-1838
Fregeur, Azelma	d. 8-2-1832 b. 12-28-1831
	d/o Alex Fregeur & Lucie Leblanc
Gabriel, Robert	d. 11-20-1754 (soldier)
Gail, Joseph	d. 5-1-1835 age 22 or 23 yrs.
Gail, M.	d. 12-9-1837
Gaille, Charles	d. 7-8-1813 age 58 yrs.
Gamelin, (child)	d. 9-17-1788 s/o Pierre Gamelin
Gamelin, -----	d. 3-15-1837 age 4 yrs.
	(Little girl of the prairie)
Gamelin, Claude	d. 3-27-1790 age 2½ yrs.
Gamelin, Laurent	d. 8-29-1788 age 2 mo.
Gamelin, Marguerite	d. 9-3-1788 age 1½ mo.
	d/o Antoine Gamelin & Magdeleine Hunot
Gamelin, Paul "Pead"	d. 11-7-1792 age 36 yrs.
Gamelin, Pierre "Prairie"	d. 2-2-1837 age 55 yrs.
Gamelin, Ursula (Lasalle)	d. 10-23-1813 age 58 yrs.
	w/o Pierre Gamelin
Ganichou see: Toulon	
Ganier, Louis	d. 8-5-1803 age 80 yrs. or more
Ganiolais, Alex	d. 3-12-1795 age 68 yrs.
Garcia, Jean	d. 8-25-1802 (spaniard)
Garretier, Marie Benan (Chartier)	d. 7-17-1835 age 44yrs.
Garriepie, Amable	d. 7-20-1790 age 35 yrs.
Gauder,------ see: Dany, (boy)	
Gauder, Toussaint	d. 10-30-1792 age 46 yrs.
Gaudere, ------	d. 2-15-1793 b. 2-15-1793
	c/o Mme Toussaint Gaudere
Gaudere, Felecite	d. 2-25-1795 b. 11-20-1773 age 23 yrs.
	w/o Alexandre Valle
Gaudere, Louis	d. 6-15-1794 age 55 yrs.
Gaudere, Louis	d. 1-11-1795 b. 2-8-1770 age 25 yrs.
	s/o Louis Gaudere & Barbe Metayer
Gaudere, Rene	d. 2-9-1793 age 57 yrs.
	h/o Catherine Compot
Gauthier, Charles see: St Marie, Felecite	
Geille see: Gaille	
Genereaux, Francois	d. 8-11-1835 age 2 mo.
	s/o Francois Genereaux & Celeste Boucher
Germain see: La Feuillade - St Germain	
Germain, Therese see: Cornoiller, antoine - Cornoiller, Claude	
Germain, (child)	d. 9-28-1837 father lives near Mr Moore
Germain, Got	d. 10-14-1838
Gettins, (child)	d. 9-6-1836
Geulleme, Marie	d. 10-13-1790 (an English girl)
Gill, Marie See: Mete, Marie Judith	
Girard, Marie see: Cardinal dit Lajeoyer, Toussaint	
Giroud, Barbe	d. 4-24-1798 age 8 mo.
Giroult, Laurent	d. 7-28-1800 age 26 or 28 yrs.
Glass, Marguerite	d. 6-10-1833 (Germans recently from Europe)
	w/o Pierre Glass

Glass, Pierre   d. 6-10-1833 (Germans recently from Europe)
                          h/o Marguerite Glass
Godaire, Francois   see: Bono, Marie
Godaire, Peter   see: Deligne, Francoise
Goddaire, Pierre   d. 4-24-1819 age 2½ yrs.
                          s/o Andre Goddaire & Ursula Goddaire
Godder, J.B.   d. 10-19-1820 age 40 yrs.
Godere, (girl)   d. 7-21-1799 b 7-21-1799
                          d/o Henri Godere & Francoise Desnoyer
Godere, Agnes   d. 12-6-1750 (drowned, Quiatanon)
                          d/o Francois Godere & Agnes Richard
Godere, Barbe   d. 10-7-1800 age 18 mo.
Godere dit Panard, Catherine d. 7-29-1796 w/o ----- Panard
Godere, Joseph   d. 9-15-1787 b. 5-22-1786 age 6 mo.
Godere, Josette   see: Boulon, (girl)
Godere, Louis   see: Leveron, Barbe
Godere, Marie Josephe   d. 7-12-1794 b. 5-16-1768 age 26 yrs.
                          w/o Honore' Dany
Godere, Marie   d. 9-2-1796 w/o -----Drouet de Richardville
Godere, Marie   d. 1820 w/o Francois Cadoret
Godere, Pierre   d. 5-26-1789 see: Codere, Pierre
Godere, Theresa   see: Edeline, Victoire
Godere dit Panard, Therese d. 5-12-1796 age 1 yr.
Godere, Ursule   d. 11-12-1756
                          d/o Francois Godere & Agnes Richard
Golman, Jean   d. 10-17-1819 age 50 yrs.
Gonzales, Angelique   d. 6-19-1801 age 19 mo.
Gonzales, Francois see: Dupre, Eloise
Goyaux, Richard   see: Dejean, Marie
Graeter, (boy)   d. 8-7-1819 age 14 days
                          s/o Christian Graeter & Marguerite Meclore
Grammer, Henry   d. 10-14-1837 age 64
                          (a German; arrived 2 days ago)
Grandmaison, Jean Bte   d. 9-6-1787 age 80 yrs.
Green, Mary Magdeline "Polly" d. 9-1-1831 age 31 yrs.
                          w/o George W. Green
Grimard, -----   see: Boyer, Marie
Grimard, Charles   d. 3-15-1835 age 60 yrs.
Grimard, Nicolas   d. 1-21-1793 age 13 yrs.
Grimard, Pierre   d. 10-13-1798 b. 9-27-1797
Grimard, Rene   d. 3-13-1802 age 32 yrs.
Grimare, (child)   d. 2-16-1833 age 1 yr.
                          c/o Jean Bte Grimare
Gueles, Adelaide   d. 11-29-1800 age 2 yrs.
Gueles, Helene   d. 11-1-1796 w/o Charles Gueles Jr.
Gueles, Ursule   d. 6-XX-1803 age 21 yrs. drowned Wabash River
Guerousse, Heleine   d. 2-12-1786 age 5 yrs.
Guerosse dit St Pierre, Therese d. 9-2-1788 age 6 yrs.
Guilbault, Catherine see: Arseneaut dit Durand, Marie Josephe
Guielle, (child)   d. 2-25-1793 b. 2-25-1793 c/o Mme Guielle
Guillaume, Augustin   d. 1-3-1799 b. 12-15-1798
                          s/o John Guillaume & Rebecca-----
Guillmore, Jean   d. 11-27-1786 age 12 days
Guindre, Dagnaux de   d. 6-13-1799

Guiolet, Jean	d. 2-17-1789 age 66 yrs.
Guionet, Marie	d. 1-4-1801
	w/o Jacques Millet dit Latrimouille
Gyroux, Therese	d. 8-3-1835 age 25 yrs.
	w/o Andre Gyroux
Hamon, Jean	d. 9-17-1754
Hamtramck, Colonel	see: Edeline, Marie
Hamtramck, Henriette	d. 5-7-1792
	d/o Jean Francois Emmetremeque(Hamtramck) & Marie Edeline
D' Harpin, (girl)	d. 2-26-1793 age 4 mo.
	d/o Poitvain D'Harpin & Geneieve Perrone
Harpin, Francoise	d. 10-11-1788 age 7½ mo.
Harpin, Pierre	d. 9-24-1788 age 10 yrs.
Harpin, Therese	d. 11-9-1800 d/o Joseph Harpin
Hearter, Drodai	see: Taylor, Eleanor
Hecthrop, Peggy	see: Brady, Catherine
Heintz, Joseph	d. 6-10-1833 (of Cholera) age 4 yrs.
Heintz, Jacob	d. 6-11-1833 (of Cholera) age 6 yrs.
Heintz, Catherine	d. 6-8-1833 (of Cholera) age 7 y-3m-7d.
	d/o Jacques Heintz & Catherine Pucomeyer
Hopkins, Guillaume joseph	d. 8-12-1788 age 6 days
Houdou, Francois	d. 9-8-1795 (schoolmaster of village)
Houellet	see: Quellet
Hunaud dit Pitoune, Victoire	d. 9-14-1802 age 15 mo.
	d/o Gabriel Hunaud dit Pitoune
Huno, Pelagie	d. 1-5-1832 age 30 Yrs. w/o Francois Troque
Hunaux, Joseph	d. 8-7-1835 age 38 yrs.
	h/o Geneieve Bohomme
Hunot, Magdeleine	see: Gamelin, Marguerite
Hunot, Marie Joseph	d. 8-29-1788 age 4 yrs.
Hunot, Michel	d. 5-13-1837
Hurtebize, Zakarie	d. 10-23-1793 age 59 yrs.
Jalbert, Charles	d. 7-21-1820 age 9 yrs.
	s/o Charles Jalbert & Marie Senet
Jalbert, Marie	d. 7-22-1820
Jalbert, Francoise	d. 10-25-1820 age 20 mo.
	d/o Charles Jalbert & Marie Senet
Jalebert, Angelique	see: Racine, Cecile
Jalebert, Jean	d. 6-18-1831 age 70 yrs.
Jenkins, (girl)	d. 9-15-1838 d/o Rosalie Jenkins
Jenkins, Rosalie (Leveille)	d. 5-2-1838
Joach	see: Raindeau
Jones, Julie	d. 11-28-1820 age 1 yr.
Jones, Mars	d. 9-24-1787 age 7 mo.
Jones William	d. 4-14-1820 age 6 mo.
	s/o William Jones & Suzanne Dubois
Jones, Robert	d. 10-1-1813 age 52 yrs. (Irishman)
Joyal, Jean Bte	see: La Fleur, Angelique

Joyal dit Lafreniere, Jean Bte   d. 12-2-1795
Joyeuse, Pierre   d. 8-23-1835 age 6 mo.
                s/o Guillaume Joyeuse & Josette Delille

Kara, Heneine dit   see: Panis, Jacques
Kelly, Hugh   d. 4-29-1820 age 57 yrs.
Kellprey, Abigail   d. 8-28-1799 age 36 to 40 yrs. (Irish)
Kemins, Katy   d. 10-14-1820 age 3 yrs.
                d/o Henry Kemins & Sally --------

La Bonte, Noe   d. 2-19-1837 age 6 yrs.
La Belle, Euphrasie   d. 1-12-1795 age 40 yrs.
                w/o Jean Bte Dubois
La Chine   see: Du Devoir
Lachine, Mme(miscarriage) 2-25-1793 from small pox
Lachine Du Devoir, (child) d. 1-16-1792
                c/o Mr. Lachine Du Devoir & Charlotte Boyer
La Coste Languedoc, Andre   d. 3-9-1793 age 66 yrs.
La Coste dit Languedoc, Charles   see: Miyot, Feleicite
La Coste, Madeleine   see: Binet, Toussaint - Binette, Jean Bte
La Course, Charlotte   see: Laffont, (boy)
La Croix, Jacques   d. 10-4-1797 b. 3-31-1711
La Croix, Louis   d. 3-20-1820 age 97 yrs.
La Croix, Marie Louise   see: Racine, Pelagie
Laderoute   see: Saguien, Sequin
Laderoute, (child)   d. 7-19-1835 age 2 yrs.
                c/o Louis Laderoute
Laderoute, Marie Elizabeth d. 12-17-1808 age 36 yrs.
                w/o Francois Boyer
Laderoutte, Madame   see: Pany, Janaux
La Douceur, (male)   d. 10-9-1798 age 22 or 24 yrs.
Lafeuilliade   see: Lefeuilliade
La Feuillade dit Bonscouyou, Francois d. 8-2-1793
La Feuillade dit Germain, Louis d. 8-2-1793
La Feuliad, Baptiste   d. 9-30-1790 age 30 yrs.
Laffont, (boy)   d. 5-23-1787 age 2 mo.
                s/o Sr Jean Laffont (surgeon) &
                Charlotte La Course
Lafforet, Pierre   d. 1-5-1819 age 82 yrs.
La Fleur   see: Dutramble
La Fleur, Angelique   d. 2-25-1789 age 55 yrs.
                w/o Jean Bte Joyal
La Fontaine, Etiemme   see: St Aubin, Catherine
La Fontenne, Charles   d. 4-10-1814 age 47 yrs.
Laforet, Archange   see: Barbeau, Francois
Laforet, Julie   d. 7-20-1835 age 30 yrs.
                w/o Ambroise Cartier
La Foret, Marie Joseph d. 2-2-1794 age 20 yrs.
La Framboise, Jean Bte   d. 7-15-1756
                s/o Antoine La Framboise & Marie (indian)
La France, Claude   d. 10-28-1755
Lagarde, Dominique   d. 9-4-1835 age 45 yrs.
                h/o Susanne Deguele

Lafreniere   see: Joyal
Lafuirse - Cheniere, Elizabeth   d. 12-16-1837
                w/o Joseph Deslauriers
La Guerre   see: Domean
Lajeoye   see: Cardinal
Lajeunesse   see: Andre
La Lumiere   see: Petit
Lami   see: Bourdeleau
Lamiraude   see: Turpin
Lamirande, Mme   d. 3-22-1837
Lamote, Cecile   see: Chappard, Jacques
Lamothe, Joseph   d. 12-18-1796 (froze to death)
Lamouraux dit Leforgeron, (child) d. 8-15-1788
                c/o Joseph Lamouroux dit Laforgeron (receipt)
Lamouraux, (child)   9-15-1788 age 6 yrs.
Lamoureux, Marie Josp   d. 8-13-1788 age 20 mo.
Lamy dit Bordeleau, Francoise d. 11-6-1800
Landaus, Andre   see: Campeau, Agathe
Landaux, Charles   d. 7-4-1791
                s/o Charles Landaux & Felicite
                        Mienyotte (Mignaux)
Langaumois   see: Rambault
Langdot, Elizabeth   d. 9-10-1835 age 2 yrs.
                d/o Louis Langdot & Francoise Delorier
Langlois, Catherine   d. 9-12-1814 age 38 yrs.
                w/o Alexandre Vallee
Langlois   see: Vallee, Susanne - Valle, Pierre
Langlois, Marie   see: Dubois, Elizabeth
Langlois, Rene   d. 2-22-1796
Languedoc, (child)   d. 6-21-1835 b. 6-21-1835
Languedoc, Elizabeth   d. 8-15-1820 age 8 yrs.
                d/o Charles Languedoc & Lusalle Bordelau
Languedoc, Mrs.   d. 6-21-1835 (?Francoise Deloeiere?)
                w/o Louis Languedoc
Languedoc, Francois   see: Compagnot, Therese
Languedoc, Jeanette   d. 4-22-1837 (child)
Languedoc, Joseph   d. 6-17-1820 age 3 weeks
                s/o Charles Languedoc & Julie Cardinal
Languedoc, Lasalle   see: Troquet, Francois
Languedoc, Michel   d. 4-28-1837 age 9 yrs.
                s/o Francois Languedoc & Therese Compagnotte
La Pierre   see: La de Boyenly
La Plante, Joseph   d. 8-22-1835 b. 1756 age 79 yrs.
                h/o late Charlotte Dubroil
Laplante, Marie Joseph   d. 9-8-1798 b. some days before
La Plante, Jean Bte   d. 10-16-1837 b. 1802 age 35 yrs.
Lapointe, Catherine   d. 6-7-1800
                w/o Louis Boyer dit Courteau
Lapointe, Joseph   d. 11-3-1777
Lardois, Catherine   see: Alard, Victoire
La Rocher, Sem   see: Campau, Jeanne
La Rue, Archange   d. 9-5-1785 age 18 days
La Rue, Catherine   d. 3-17-1790 age 19 yrs.
Lasalle, Ursula   see: Gamelin, Ursula

Lassele, Nicholas   d. 4-20-1812 age 50 yrs.
Lasselle, Oliver   d. 1-3-1812 age 3 yrs.
Latour, (child)   d. 3-23-1793 age 3 yrs. c/o Pierre Latour &
                                Geneieve Trempé dit Cournouailler
Latour, Jean Bte   d. 12-4-1820 age 1 yr.
Latourre, Pierre   d. 10-2-1788 age 1 y. 5 m. 4 d.
La Tremouille, Jacques   see: Le Fleur, Marie
Latremouille, Jean Bte   d. 3-4-1820 age 5 yrs.
                                s/o Jean Bte Latremouille &
                                Victoire Tirot - Girard
Latrimouille, Francois   d. 2-9-1793 b. 12-8-1784 age 9 yrs.
                                s/o Jacques Latrimouille &
                                Marie Derosiers dit La Fleur
La Vigne, Catherine   d. 7-29-1791 age 59 yrs.
                                w/o Charles Pottie Lardoise
Lavigne dit Texier, Francois d. 11-27-1800 age 4 mo.
La Violette See: Touga, Tougas
Laviolette dit Violon, -----Mme d. 6-7-1838
Lavalette, Clothide   see: Deslorier, Pierre
Laviolette, Marie   see: Troquet, Jeannette - Troquet, Louis -
                                Barnabe, Charles Jean
Leblanc, Lucie   see: Fregeur, Azelma
Le Coste dit Languedoc, Andre   see: Custas, Joseph
Le de Boyenly, Joseph (Pierre ou Jean) d. 7-16-1765 or 1766
Ledike, -----Pohaise Catherine d. 1777 w/o -----Ubue
Le Duc, Catherine   d. 3-6-1785 age 70 yrs.
                                w/o late Francis Millet
Le Fleur, Marie   d. 1-3-1801 w/o Jacques La Tremoille
Lefeuilliade, Jelles du May d. X-18-1765
Lefeuvre dit Belon, Charles d. 9-10-1777
Lefeuvre, Antoine   see: Quere, Marie
Lefeuvre, Antoine   d. 10-5-1792 age 6 yrs.
                                s/o Antoine Lefeuvre &
                                Josette Querie dit La Toulipe
Lefeuvre dit Chapeau, Antoine   see: Carron, Marie Louise
Lefeuvre, Marie Louise   see: Dutramble, Felicite
Lefeuvre dit Chapeau, Pierre d. 11-5-1798 age 6 or 7 yrs.
Leforgeron   see: Lamourauh
Lefeniere   see: Joyal
Lefuirse - Chinierie, Elizabeth d. 12-16-1837
                                w/o Joseph Deslauriers
Le Grand, Francois   d. 10-1-1788 age 2 y. 11 m. 3 d.
Legrand, Gabriel Jr.   d. 12-5-1789 age 21 yrs.
Legrand, Gabriel Sr. Esquire d. 2-9-1789 age 68 yrs.
Le Gras, Sieur Jean Marie Philippe d. 2-8-1788 age 54 yrs.
                                Colonel - Militia of Vincennes
Le Gras, Jean Marie Philippe d. 7-15-1786??
Le Gras, Jean Marie Philippe see: Devegnet, Marie
Leneveux, Jean   d. 12-23-1790 age 40 yrs.
Leonardy, Pierre (Lt.) d. 11-24-1753 b. 11-4-1720
                                s/o Jean Henry Leonardy & Jeanne Foco
Leris   see: roy
L'Etang, Jean Bte   d. 1-3-1796 on the bank of the Wabash
                                while hunting - he was buried there.

Le Tremouille, Jacques Millet dit d. 12-25-1800 b. 1734
Leuvar dit Belorny, Charle d. 9-18-1777
Leveille, Geneieve   d. 1-7-1839 age 26 yrs.
                            d/o Louis Leveille & Rose
Leveron   see: Metayer
Leveron, Amirante   d. 2-26-1835 age 75 yrs.
                            w/o ----- Turpin
Leveron, Charlotte   see: Malet, Jean Bte - Mallet, Marguerite
Leveron dit Metayer, Joseph d. 1-30-1771 age 50 yrs.
Leveron dit Metayer, Louis d. 3-12-1795 age 68 yrs.
Levron, Barbe   d. 9-11-1798 w/o Louis Godere
Levron, Joseph   d. 2-11-1796
Levy, Francois Xavier   d. 10-8-1800 age 7 mo.
--- lionnais,-----   d. 11-8-1761
Lionnoise, Marie Victoire   d. 9-4-1788 age 6 yrs.
Litalien   see: Andray
Litalien, Mme   2-25-1793 - Miscarrage from small pox
Litalien, Marie Joseph   d. 4-1-1793 age 32 yrs.
Lognon, Francois   d. 12-24-1796
Lognon, Joseph   d. 9-11-1799 age 11 mo.
Lognon, Louis   d. 2-5-1819 b. 5-2-1818
                            s/o Louis Lognon & Henriette Cardinal
Lognon, Nicolas   d. 10-17-1803 age 18 mo.
Loiseau, Francois   d. 3-22-1757 (soldier)
Lours   see: Bergan

Mac Mallony, Thomas   d. 10-5-1838
Mahoney,-----   d. 2-19-1835 age 70s River Dechess
                            son in law of, M. Clements
Mahoney, Benedict   d. 10-29-1831 age 36 yrs.
                            h/o Jane White
Mahoney, Francois   d. 9-5-1838 age 34 yrs.
                            (of La Cheminee de Pierre)
Maisonville, Joseph   see: Despointes, Geneieve
Major   see: Beutron
Malet, Jean Bte   d. 9-12-1788 age 2 y. 2 m. 9 d.
Malet, Jean Bte   d. 2-20-1793 age 5 yrs.
                            s/o Francois Malet & Charlotte Levron
Malet, Louis   d. 6-14-1794 age 60 yrs.
Malet, Louis   d. 12-24-1800 age 17½ mo.
Mallet,-----Mrs.   d. 1825
Mallet, (boy)   d. 4-25-1793 Illinois - bur Kaskaskia?
                            s/o Pierre Mallet & Marie Angelique Bautron
Mallet, Benoit Josephe   d. 9-27-1794 age 17 mo. 3 days
Mallet, Eleanore (Miss)   d. 9-7-1837 age 17 yrs.
Mallet, Elizabeth   see: Richard, Francoise - Richard, Jean Bte
Mallet, Francis   see: Le Duc, Catherine
Mallet, Francois   d. 9-15-1835 age 16 yrs.
                            orphan - living with Antoine Cartier
Mallet, Heleine   d. 9-24-1788 age 5 yrs.
Mallet, Joseph   d. 2-6-1793 age 5 mo.
                            s/o Louis Mallet & Louise Crepon

Mallet, Marguerite	d. 10-10-1790
	d/o Antoine Mallet & Catherine Bordeau
Mallet, Marguerite	d. 11-1-1792
	d/o Francois Mallet & Charlotte Levron
Mallet, Marie	d. 3-20-1791 age 2 yrs.
	d/o Pierre Mallet &
	Angelique Beutron dit Major
Mallet, Therese	d. 9-19-1763 w/o ??
Mallet, Therese	d. 3-17-1790 age 11 yrs.
Mallet, Ursule	d. 10-10-1787 age 14 mo.
Mallett, Angelique	d. 1-6-1814 age 2 yrs. 3 mo.
Maloin, -----	d. 8-19-1786 age 28 or 29
Marchall, Ant	d. 3-1-1816
Marie,-----	d. 10-15-1797 age 27 mo.
Marie, Josette	d. 12-27-1750
	w/o Julian Trottier dit Desriviers
Marie, Josette see: Desriviers, Julian	
Marie Marguerite	d. 10-23-1800 (widow)
Martin, Etienne (Stephen?)	d. 4-16-1770
Mastou, Pierre	d. 1-12-1757
Meclore, Marguerite see: Graeter, (boy)	
Meeni, Jean	d. 6-22-1801 (Irishman-soldier of Fort)
Melayer see: Perron	
Meloche, Marie see: De Lile, Francoise	
Meloche, Marie Joseph	d. 1-22-1793 age 37 yrs.
	w/o Amable De Lile
Menard, Phillipe	d. 10-2-1788 age 20 yrs. 6 mo.
Meny, Antoine	d. 2-26-1793 age 57 yrs.
Messin, Pierre	d. 1-5-1757 (soldier)
Metay, Antoine	d. 10-30-1800 age 40 yrs.
Metay, Charles see: Benac,-----	
Metay, Louis	d. 12-14-1802 age 8 yrs.
Metay, N.	d. 10-29-1836 age 15 yrs. (of Cathernettes)
Metay, Rene	d. 9-22-1793
Metayer see: Leveron	
Metayer dit Leveron, (girl)	d. 10-2-1793
	d/o Joseph Metayer dit Leveron &
	Cecile Cardinal
Metayer, Barbe see: Gaudere, Louis	
Metayer dit Leveron, Joseph	d. 1-12-1795 age 9 yrs.
	s/o Joseph Metayer dit Leveron &
	Celeste Milliete (Cardinal)
Metayer, Marie	d. 3-15-1789 age 55 yrs. (a Piankichias)
	w/o Louis Metayer
Mete, Catherine	d. 8-8-1837 age 44 yrs. (of Catherinettes)
	w/o Louis Boyer
Mete, Marie Judith	d. 9-4-1831
	d/o Joseph Mete & Marie Gill
Metta, Marie Louise	d. 8-16-1809
Mette, Magdeleine	d. 5-17-1831 w/o Martial Mondou
Michel, Laurent	d. 10-10-1802 age 18 mo.
	s/o Francois Michel
Mienyotte (Mignaux), Felicite see: Landaux, Charles	
Mignaux, Pierre	d. 5-21-1790 age 50 yrs.

```
Milhome or Millson, Jean Bte   see: Paupart, Mabel Josephe
Millet dit Latrimouille Jacques see: Guionet, Marie
Millet, Frances   see: Le Duc, Catherine
Miners, William              d. 3-31-1835
Mizote, Felicite             d. 12-21-1794 age 40 yrs.
                             w/o Charles LaCoste dit Languedoc
Momeni, Magloire Joseph      d. 7-4-1835 age 3 mo.
Momeny, (child)              d. 10-4-1838 ( of Catherinettes)
Mominy, (child)              d. 7-13-1837 age 3 mo.
Mominy, (child)              d. 9-15-1838
Mominy, (boy)                d. 1-4-1838 age 3 yrs.
                             s/o Antoine Mominy
Mondou, Martial   see: Mette, Magdeleine
Montmirel   see: Durand
Montmirel, Joseph            d. 12-30-1790
                             s/o Joseph Montmirel & Josette Thiebault
Montplasier, Andre           d. 12-28-1803 (adult)
Montplasier, Magdeleine   see: Dutour, Pierre
Moore, Jean                  d. 9-13-1838 age 13 yrs.
Moore, Laurence              d. 10-20-1794 age 36 yrs.
                             Irishman - master of the English School
Moore, William               d. 11-3-1837 age 2 mo.
                             s/o Miss Moore
Morel, Jean Bte              d. 2-16-1793 age 29
                             s/o ----- Morel & ----- Dubois
Morphee, Jean                d. 2-20-1789 age 3 mo.
Mousette, Michelle           d. 10-15-1813 age 30 yrs.
Moyse, Barbe                 d. 7-XX-1823
Moyse, Francoise             d. 9-18-1800 age 7 mo.
Moyse, Jean Bte              d. 9-20-1799 age 11 mo.
Moyse, Joseph                d. 10-9-1802 age 18 mo.
                             s/o Charles Moyse
Murphi, John                 d. 3-20-1838 (fo Washington, Daviess Co.
Murry, Daniel                d. 9-14-1820 age 28 yrs. (Irishman)
Myers, Napoleon              d. 4-15-1820 age 14 mo.


Nicencyn??, M.               d. 8-20-1838
                             brother in law of Mr Thorn
Noland, Henry                d. 3-19-1835
Normy, -----Mr.              d. 10-18-1838


Oizi   see: Dizi
Oizi or Dizi, Michel   see: Du Devoir, Barbe
Orleans, Angelique           d. 2-21-1791 age 60 yrs.
                             w/o Philbert Orleans
Oualette, Charlotte          d. 4-26-1803
                             w/o J.B. Duchene dit Conisant
Ouelete, Charlotte see: Duchaine dit Conisant, Marie
Ouellet, Brigitte            d. 12-29-1788 age 2 yrs.
Outlas, Francoise            d. 11-28-1801
                             widow of Ambroise Dagenaise
```

Page, Guillaume	d. 2-2-1801 age 60 yrs.
Page, Joseph	d. 2-21-1800 age 29 or 30 yrs.
Page, Madeleine	d. 3-19-1803 age 18 yrs. w/o Hiacynthe Desjardens married just 2 mo. before
Paget, Catherine	d. 11-17-1798 w/o Gme Paget
Paget, Dominique see: Villeneuve, Marie	
Pakane, Marie & Child	d. 2-10-1793 age 37 yrs. w/o J.B. Boneau
Pakane, Antoine	d. 1-14-1793
Pallu, Marie Anne see: De Noyone, Louis	
Panard see: Godere, Catherine	
Panis, (boy)	d. 5-14-1792 s/o Etienne Panis & Marie Sara
Panis, Jacques	d. 2-15-1793 age 45 yrs. h/o Helen dit Kara?
Panneton, Etienne	d. 2-4-1803 age 55 yrs.
Pany, Janaux	d. 10-13-1789 age 30 yrs. (of Madame le Deroute)
Paquin, Agathe	d. 10-14-1788 age 1yr 7 mo.
Paudevin, Catherine	d. 4-21-1812 age 20 yrs. w/o Louis St Germain
Paudevin, Joseph	d. 9-3-1813 age 12
Paupart, Mabel Josephe	d. 11-18-1766 b. 10-4-1734 w/o Jean Bapt Millson or Milhome
Pelletier, Andrew	d. 3-15-1785 age 46 yrs.
Pelletier, Antoine	d. 5-14-1789 age 8 yrs. (killed by indians)
Pelletier, Eleanor	d. 9-21-1788 age 8 mo.
Pelletier, Francois	d. 2-4-1788 age 44 yrs.
Pelletier, Geneieve	d. 4-28-1820 age 10 mo. d/o Pierre Pelletier & Barbe Cardinal
Pelletier, Marie	d. 3-1-1835 w/o Pelletier of the prairie
Pelletier, Michel	d. 10-17-1790 age 5 yrs.
Perret, Pierre	d. 2-26-1793 age 61 yrs.
Perron, Geneieve see: Harpen, (girl)	
Perron dit Melayer, Joseph	d. 1-30-1771 age 50 yrs.
Perron, Pierre	d. 12-15-1785 age 100 yrs.
Perrot, Nicolas	d. 9-25-1789 age 50 yrs.
Pettite dit La Lumiere, Antoine	d. 10-13-1788 age 2mo. 20 days
Petit, Antoine	d. 7-16-1813
Petro, Felicite	d. 9-13-1789 age 8 mo.
Philibert, Etienne	d. 4-26-1786 age 77 yrs. (buried between holy water font & the door of the Church)
Picard, Pierre Francois	d. 3-20-1831 s/o Alexis Picard & Bernice Bizayon
Pilond, N.	d. 2-19-1800
Pitoune see: Hunaud	
Poidevin, Joseph	d. 10-XX-1819 s/o Francois Xavier Poidevin & Victoire Sanson
Poitiars, Catherine see: Allard, Angelique	
Poret du Faubray, Gustave	d. 5-2-1802 age 22 mo.

Potdevin, Therese   d. 9-14-1821 age 4½ yrs.
Potevin dit Harpin, Jean d. 2-6-1797
Pottie dit Lardoise, Charles   see: La Vigne, Catherine
Powell, Elizabeth   d. 2-11-1787 (from Childbirth)
    w/o John Rice Johns
Prince, George   d. 9-28-1808 age 2½ yrs.
    s/o Sr Ouilliam Prince & Therese Tremble
Provereal, Jean Bte   d. 10-10-11794 age 64 yrs.
Prudomme, Madeleine   d. 8-15-1790 age 57 yrs.
    w/o Joseph De Ganne
Pucomeyer, Catherine   d. 1-16-1833 age 32 yrs. (of Cholera)
Pucomeyer, Catherine   see: Heintz, Jacob

Quere, Marie   d. 1-14-1836 age 67 yrs.
    w/o Antoine Lefevre
Querie dit La Toulipe, Josette   see: Lefevre, Antoine
----quimont, Louis   d. 4-19-1770

Racicot, Francois   d. 5-20-1802 age 1½ mo.
Racine, Babi   see: La Fond, Marie
Racine, Cecile   d. 11-25-1831 age 18 mo.
    d/o Francois Racine & Angelique Jalibert
Racine, -----Mrs.   d. 12-7-1834 W/o M. Racine; mother of twins
Racine St Marie, Jean Bte d. 6-18-1788 age 7 mo.
Racine, Jeanne   see: Barrouet, Francois
Racine, Vos   d. 9-2-1835 age 6 mo.
    s/o Pierre Racine & Adelaide Compagnot
Racine, Pelagie   d. 9-9-1790
    d/o Jean Bte Racine & Marie Louise LaCroix
Racine dit St Marie, Pierre d. 11-12-1809 age 45 yrs.
Racine, Suzanne   see: Baron, Toussaint
Racuse Francois   d. 2-15-1819
    s/o Samuel Racuse & Marie Jeanne Campeau
Raindeau dit Joach, Jacques d. 3-23-1778
Rambault dit Langaumois, Andre
    d. 3-1-1778 (found dead at his home)
Range, Marguerite   d. 12-11-1790
    d/o Joseph Range & Marguerite Clairmont
Rarindeau dit Ejould, ----- ialque d. 3-22-1778?
Rasalie or Ravolet, Marie Louise d. 4-10-1770
    d/o Jean Bte Rasalde & Marie Francoise
                      Fauvel Tusan
Raux, Joseph   d. 10-11-1791 age 53 yrs.
Ravalet dit Bouissard, Andre d. 10-16-1794 age 6 mo.
Ravalet, Antoine   d. 3-25-1813 age 54 yrs.
Ravalet, Francoise   see: Bono, Francois
Ravalette, Brisard   d. 6-27-1835 age 3 yrs.
    s/o Louis Ravalette
Ravalette, Francois   d. 12-20-1834 (of Cathérinettes)
Ravalette, Helene   d. 12-26-1800 age 22 mo.
Ravalette, Ismael   d. 9-30-1820 age 3 mo.
    s/o Louis Ravalette & Helen Campeau

Ravalette, Magdelaine	d. 11-7-1798 w/o Joseph De Gane
Ravalette, Michel	d. 10-7-1818 age 1 yr.
	s/o Louis Ravalette & Helen Campeau
Ravalette, Marie	d. 11-1-1832 age 18 mo.
Ravalette, Marie Anne	d. 8-26-1821 age 13 mo.
Renaud see: Des Lauriers	
Ranaud, Charlotte	d. 12-17-1802
	w/o Joseph Chartier (widow Ducharme)
Renaud, Marguerite	d. 7-14-1795 age 3 or 4 yrs.
	d/o Jean Bte Renaud & savage woman
Ranaud dit Desloriers, Victoire	d. 2-7-1793 age 1½ yrs.
	s/o Jean Bte Renaud & Magdeleine Bordeleau
Rene, N.(of the Prarie)	d. 2-25-1835 age 65 yrs.
Richard, (child)	d. 8-31-1838 age 1 mo.
Richard, Agnes	d. 1-9-1803 age 18 yrs. (Terre Haute)
Richard, Agnes see: Godere, Agnes - Godere, Ursule	
Richard, Francois	d. 7-19-1789 age 2½ yrs.
	s/o Jean Bte Richard & Elizabeth Mallet
Richard, Jean Bte	d. 9-25-1790 age 8 mo.
	s/o Baptiste Richard & Elizabeth Mallet
Richard, Pierre	d. 8-15-1797 age 3 yrs.
Richardville, (child)	d. 8-19-1838
	c/o Mr H. Richardville
Richardville, Antoine	d. 7-27-1824
Richardville see: Godere, Marie	
Richardville, Mme Drouet de - miscarriage - 2-25-1793 from small pox	
Richardville, Antoine	d. 11-1-1831 age 70 or 72 yrs.
Richardville, Antoine Drouet de Jr.	
	d. 10-7-1802 age 23 yrs.
Richardville, Henri de	d. 11-21-1837
Richardville, Jean B. Drouet de	d. 5-9-1838 b. 8-18-1871
Richardville, Jean Bte Jr. see: Bonhomme, Marianne	
Richardville, Francoise Drouet de	d. 4-9-1800
	widow of Francois Riday dit Bosseron
Richardville, Marie Louise	d. 5-28-1831
	w/o Michel Brouett (Brouillet)
Richerville, Antoine Drouet de	d. 4-15-1765
Richerville, Marie see: Brouillet, Elizabeth	
Riday dit Bosseron, Francois see: Richardville, Francoise Drouet de	
Riendeau, Louis	d. 9-15-1787 age 11 mo.
Robert, Gabriel	d. 11-20-1754 (soldier)
Robineau, Louis	d. 9-7-1836 age 13 yrs.
Rivet, ----- Mr.	d. 2-28-1804 ??
Rochard, Mme see: Sapa, Francoise	
Room dit Descarraux, Andre	d. 10-9-1800 age 30 yrs.
Roussian, Ursule	d. 9-20-1799 age 18 mo.
Roux, Antoinette	d. 9-11-1795 age 4 mo.
Roy dit Leris, Louis	d. 4-10-1812 b. 1786 age 26 yrs.
Russell, Robert see: Cartier, Susanne	
Samson, Barbe	d. 10-18-1788 age 3 mo.
Sanacrerre, Jean Bte	d. 12-6-1755

Sanson, Victorie   see: poidevin, Joseph
Sanspeur, Pierre   d. 4-17-1794 age 75 yrs.
Santa Anna, Julien   d. 2-15-1802 (Mexican)
                          died leagues from Fort Vincennes
Santier, Charles Louis Oliver (Dr.) d. 9-13-1781
Sapa, Francoise   d. 12-24-1794 age 18 yrs.
                          (savage woman raised by Mme Rochard
Saquien dit Laderoute, Nicholas d. 1-29-1795 age 18 or 19 yrs.
Sara, Marie   see: Panis, (boy)
Sauxerre, Jean Bte   d. 12-6-1755
Schnepp, Madeleine   d. 10-4-1837
Senet, Marie see: Jalbert, Charles - Jalbert, Francois
Sequin, Barbe see: Boyer, Charles - Boyer, Marie
Sequin, Jean Bte   d. 9-24-1798 age 2 yrs.
Sequin dit Laderoute, Louis -.d. 2-10-1802
Severe, Martha   d. 1-21-1801   w/o Louis Severe
Severe, Louis   d. 5-22-1809 age 60 yrs.
Sheridan, Michael   d. 3-19-1837
Shicott, Marie   d. 7-26-1831 (orphan)
Sigaud le Fleur   see: Dutremble
Simms, Joseph M.   d. 5-18-1837 age 15 yrs. 9 mo. (Shelbyville)
                          s/o Joseph M. Simms & Tabatha
Simon, -----Mrs.   d. 12-26-1836 age 55 yrs.
Smake, Francois   d. 7-23-1802 bpt 5-18-1802
Smith, Fanny   d. 10-26-1808 age 14 mo.
                          d/o Charles Smith (merchant)
Soligne, Brigette   d. 8-10-1835 age 25 days
                          d/o Joseph Soligne & Jeanne Bono
Souligne, (child)   d. 10-24-1837 age "some months"
Souligny, Marianne   d. 3-22-1831 age 23
                          w/o Isaac Watson
Souligny, Marriannae   see: Watson, Jean Leon
St Amand, Marie Magdeleine d. 3-5-1753 age 55 yrs.
                          w/o Alexis Carrie
St Aubin, Catherine   d. 1-25-1796
                          w/o Etienne La Fontaine (her last Husband)
Ste Marie   see: Racine
Ste Marie, Felicite   d. 3-24-1831 w/o Charles Gauthier
Ste Marie, Joseph   d. 5-31-1786 age 84 yrs.
Ste Marie, Marie Louise   d. 8-2-1788 age 10 mo.
Stewart, (child)   d. 7-8-1835 b. 7-8-1835
Stewart, (girl)   d. 2-2-1838 age 14 yrs.
St Germain, Louis Mr.   d. 7-20-1838
St Germain, Louis see: Paudevin, Catherine
St Germain, Pierre   d. 4-13-1787 age 66 yrs.
St Germain, Pierre   d. 2-16-1813 age 30 yrs.
St Jean   see: Tirard
St Marie, (child)   d. 8-1-1788
                          s/o Joseph St Marie (receipt)
St Marie, Angelique Louise d. 9-9-1788 age 7 yrs.
St Marie, Ceclie   d. 2-7-1833 age 27
                          w/o Charles Gauthier
Stout, Jean Elihu   d. 9-17-1837 age 2 yrs. 2 mo.
St Pierre   see: Guerousse

Tabbs, Charles   d. 9-11-1820 age 8 yrs.
                                  s/o Moses Tabbs & Jeannette Marie Carroll
Taylor, Eleanor   d. 11-6-1832 age 9 yrs. 4 mo.
                                  d/o Johnston Taylor & Drodai Hearter
Tesier, Francois   d. 8-28-1819 age 60 yrs.
Texier see: Lavigne
Theriaque, Laurent   d. 2-22-1803 age 2 mo.
Theriaque, Therese   d. 10-5-1800 age 8½ mo.
Thiebault, Josette see: Montmirel, Joseph
Thierry, Julien   d. 8-31-1797 (of bloody flux)
Thomas, Elias (Mrs)   d. 9-7-1838
Thorn,-----Mr.   see: Nicencyn, M.
Tierry, Pierre   d. 1-4-1793 age 25 yrs.
                                  (married with widow ------Buvinet)
Tirard dit St Jean, (girl) d. 11-10-1787 age 15 mo.
                                  d/o Nicholas Tirard dit St Jean &
                                  Marie Anne Tirio
Tirard, Nicholas   d. 7-19-1793
Tirio, Marie Anne see: Tirard dit St Jean, (girl)
Toinche, Baptiste   d. 7-12-1801 age 15 mo.
                                  (savage) - tribe of Kaskaskia
Touga, Tougas see: Laviolette
Touga, Baptiste   d. 3-17-1790 age 40 yrs.
Touga, Catherine   d. 9-7-1788 age 1 yr. 10 mo.
Touga, Francoise   d. 9-11-1788 age 2 yrs. 4 mo. 8 days
Touga, Jean Bte   d. 3-10-1814 age 5 yrs.
Touga, Joseph   d. 11-3-1802 age 2 mo.
Touga, Marie Joseph   d. 7-28-1789 age 2½ yrs.
Touga, Therese   d. 9-29-1788 age 6 yrs. 5 mo. 9 days
                                  d/o Jean Bte Touga & Catherine Crepeau
Tougas dit Laviolette, Alexandre d. 8-30-1809 age 2 yrs.
                                  s/o Francoise Tougas dit Laviolette
Tougas, Isaac   d. 9-21-1792 age 9 days
                                  s/o Joseph Tougas & Jeanne Cardinal
Tougas, Leonard   d. 7-8-1791 age 2 yrs.
                                  s/o Joseph Tougas & Jeanne Cardinal
Tougas dit Laviolette, Louis d. 9-4-1787 age 7 yrs.
                                  s/o Jean Bte Tougas dit Laviolette &
                                  Catherine Crepan
Tougat dit Laviolette, Joseph d. 12-11-1793 age 53 Yrs.
Toulon dit Ganichon, Jean   d. 10-21-1795
Toulon dit Ganichon, Jean   see: Fausement?, Susan Therese
Toulon, Jean Bte   d. 2-23-1789 age 6 Mo.
Toulon, Susanne   d. 8-15-1790
                                  d/o Jean Toulon & Susanne Fausement
Toulouse, Marie Josephe see: Tremble, Louis
Trampe dit Cornoualie, Pierre d. 4-15-1793 age 54 yrs.
Tremblay, Therese   d. 10-8-1800 age 18 mo.
Tremble see: Des Rosiers & Du Rivage
Tremble, Etienne   d. 2-11-1820 age 13 Yrs.
                                  s/o Etienne Tremble
Tremble, Louis   d. 2-26-1793 age 45 yrs.
                                  h/o Mme Marie Josephe Toulouse

Tremble, Therese   see: Prince, George
Trempe dit cornouailler, Geneieve   see: Latour,----------
Trochet, (girl)   d/ 2-19-1793
                             d/o Francois Trochet & Felicite Cardinal
Troquet, Francois   d. 9-18-1831 age 2 yrs.
                             s/o Nicholas Troquet & Lasulle Languedoc
Troque, Francois   see: Huno, Pelagie
Troquet, Jeannette   d. 8-30-1835 age 1 yr.
                             d/o Paul Troquet & Marie Laviolette
Troquet, Louis   d. 5-16-1831 age 4 yrs.
                             s/o Paul Troquet & Magdeline Laviolette
Trottier dit Desriviers, Julien   see: Marie, Josette
Turpain   see: Arpains
Turpain (Arpaina), Celeste   d. 11-13-1811 age 3 yrs.
                             d/o Francois Arpains
Turpin, -----   see: Levron, Amerante
Turpin dit Lameraude, (child)   d. 2-25-1793 b. 2-25-1793
                             c/o Mme Turpin dit Lameraude
Turpin, Francois   d. 9-6-1788 age 2 yrs.
Turpin, Francois   d. 10-1-1809 age 50 yrs.
Turpin, Jean Bte   d. 8-16-1786 age 4½ yrs.
Turpin, Marie Joseph   d. 3-7-1786 age 7 mo.
Turpin, Ursule   d. 8-7-1797 age 2 yrs.
Tusan, Marie Francois Fauvel   see; Rasalee, Marie Louise

Vacher, Marie   d. 6-25-1818 age 21 yrs.
                             w/o Jean Belay
Vachette, Louis   d. 2-25-1820 age 15 days
                             s/o Francois Vachette & Francoise Delorier
Valcourt, J. Bte   d. 10-22-1818 age 40 yrs.
Valet, Ester   d. 6-20-1819 age 40 yrs.
                             w/o Pierre Lami dit Bourdeleau
Valet, Ester   see: Bordeleau, Susanne
Valiere, Alexandre   see: Bonneau, Francoise
Valiquet, Francois   d. 11-25-1786 age 7 days
Valle, (child)   d. 2-22-1795   c/o Alexandre Valle
Valle, Alexandre   see: Gaudere, Felicite
Valle, Carmelite   d. 1-XX-1824
Valle, Nicolas   d. 12-6-1792 age 2½ yrs.
Valle, Susanne   d. 12-17-1823 age 23 yrs.
                             d/o Alexandre Valle & Catherine Langlois
Valle, Victoire   d. 10-6-1833 age 32
                             w/o Jean Delisle
Vallet, Pierre   d. 10-6-1831 age 20 yrs.
                             s/o Alexandre Vallette &
                             Catherine Langlois
Vallee, Alexandre   d. 2-20-1813 age 50 yrs.
Vallee, Alexandre   see: Langlois, Catherine
Vanderburgh, Guillaume Henri   d. 12-21-1799 age 20 mo.
                             buried St Xavier Church under 2nd
                             pew in middle row.
Vaudrie, Marie Rose   d. 9-6-1788 age 5 yrs. 4 mo.

Vaudry, Amable	d. 4-24-1813 age 15 yrs.
	s/o Mme Jean Bte Vaudry
Vaudry, Antoine	d. 5-21-1795 age 17 yrs.
Vaudry, Jean Bte	d. 9-24-1792 age 70 yrs.
Vaudry, Jean Bte	d. 7-10-1793 age 32 yrs.
Vaudry, Marie	d. 1-7-1801 w/o ----- Vaudry
Veaudry, Fran	d. 10-16-1810
Villenauve, Eleanor	see: Dejean, Eleanor
Villeneuve, -----	see: andre, -----
Villeneuve, Charles	d. 12-27-1795
Villeneuve, Helene (Mme)	d. 11-28-1837
Villeneuve, Joseph	d. 4-11-1813 age 10 yrs.
Villeneuve, Marie	d. 1-14-1821 age 41 yrs.
Villeneuve, Marie	see: D'Albee, Helen
Villeneuve, Marie	d. 2-18-1820 age 30 yrs.
	w/o Dominique Paget
Vitrais, Baptiste	d. 4-21-1791 age 25 yrs.
Vlle, Charles	see: Carpentier, Dme Pelagie
Vodrille, (child)	d. 8-27-1788
	c/o Jacques Vodrille (receipts)

Wago, -----Mrs.	d. 1825
Watson, Isaac	see: Souligney, Marianne
Watson, Jean Leon	d. 7-31-1831 age 11 mo.
	s/o Isaac Watson & Marrianne Souligney
Wau, Marie Joseph	d. 10-29-1793 age 30 yrs.
	w/o Antoine Dany
Weau, Michel	d. 2-16-1793 age 66 yrs.
White, Jane	see: Mahoney, Benedict
Wilson, Jean Bte	d. 8-11-1788 age 15 days
Wilson, Marie Ann	d. 8-29-1786 age 13 days
Wilson, -----	d. 8-17-1786 (mother of Marie Ann)